Cars of the World in Color

RACING CARS
and
Record Breakers
1898-1921

by
T. R. NICHOLSON

Illustrated by
JOHN W. WOOD
Norman Dinnage
Frank Friend
Brian Hiley
William Hobson
Tony Mitchell
Jack Pelling

THE MACMILLAN COMPANY
NEW YORK

Library of Congress Catalog Card Number: 72–160080

First American Edition 1971
First published in Great Britain in 1971 by
Blandford Press Ltd, London

ACKNOWLEDGMENTS

The author is grateful to G. N. Georgano, Michael
Sedgwick and Cyril Posthumus for their comments on
the manuscript and for general help with research, and
also to the Montagu Motor Museum for certain
illustration reference.

THE MACMILLAN COMPANY
866 Third Avenue, New York NY 10022

Printed in Great Britain

INTRODUCTION

The first organized motor trial took place in July 1894 between Paris and Rouen, and the first motor race was held in the following year, when twenty-two cars made the journey from Paris to Bordeaux and back again, the winner averaging 15 m.p.h. for the 732-mile journey. At this time any vehicle which entered for a race was a racing car, whether it was a motor tricycle or a six-passenger steam brake; the specialized competition car had not yet arrived. The divergence between touring car and racing car was a gradual process, largely a matter of engine size at first, and frequently a very attractive touring vehicle could be made out of last year's model of racing car, equipped with a four-passenger body. Cars which were treated in this way included the 1901 60-h.p. Mors (7), the 1903 60-h.p. Mercedes (17), and the 1908 Itala (36). The 1898 Paris–Amsterdam–Paris race was the most significant of the early town-to-town events, not only because it was the first to cross an international frontier, but also because of the cars which took part. These included the 8-h.p. Panhard which had a four-cylinder vertical engine and steering wheel on an inclined column, both important steps forward, and the 8-h.p. Amédée Bollées (1), which had streamlined bodies specially designed for racing. Speeds had improved considerably on the 15 m.p.h. of Paris–Bordeaux three years earlier; Fernand Charron's winning Panhard averaged 26·9 m.p.h., and for a 40-mile stretch was doing 32 m.p.h. Paris–Amsterdam–Paris also saw a separate class for light cars for the first time. These were cars weighing less than 400 kg., and three years later in the Paris–Berlin race, three categories were set up: *Grandes Voitures* (Heavy Cars over 650 kg.), *Voitures Légères* (Light Cars) (400–650 kg.), and *Voiturettes* (under 400 kg.). The introduction of categories for smaller cars gave encouragement to less wealthy manufacturers and owners who could never have competed against the giants such as Panhard and Mors. For three years these three categories raced together, which in part accounts for the enormous fields of entries in the later town-to-town races. After the last of these, the uncompleted Paris–Madrid race of 1903, the classes were separated.

Engine size and power rose rapidly between 1900 and 1905; the Cannstatt-Daimler of 1899/1900 (4) developed 28 h.p. from 5·7 litres, while the Renault which won the first Grand Prix (26) had a capacity of nearly 13 litres and developed 105 b.h.p. This relative improvement in efficiency resulted from developments such as the mechanically-operated inlet valve and the replacement of the platinum tube ignition by an electric system. On the other hand engine speeds had not risen very much, and the majority of the 1906 Grand Prix power units turned at a leisurely 1200 to 1400 r.p.m. Because of this, the only path to greater power was via increased litreage, and it was not until the invaluable work of Laurence Pomeroy at Vauxhall (45), Louis Coatalen at Sunbeam (48), Ernest Henry at Peugeot (65), Michelet at Delage (52, 69), and Ettore Bugatti (51), that engine sizes began to come down. In other ways design improved

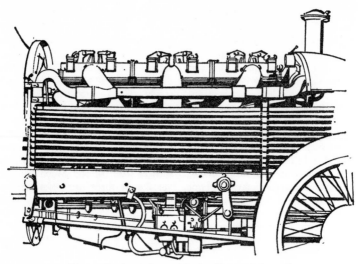

Fig. 1. Engine of 1904 Napier 'Samson' (see 18)

considerably during the first few years of the century; mechanically-operated inlet valves replaced the automatic type by 1903 on most racing cars, and magneto ignition was substituted for battery and trembler coil at about the same time, although Emile Mors, an electrical engineer before he became a car manufacturer, used a magneto from his first car of 1897. Four-speed gear-boxes were in general use and nearly all the larger cars used chains for their final drive, as it was thought that a live axle could not cope with great power, and if it was made strong enough to do so it would be very heavy. An exception was the Renault (26); Louis Renault employed shaft drive on his original *voiturette* of 1898, and when, like other makers, he increased the size of his racing cars, he remained faithful to a system which did not become universal on large cars until shortly before the

First World War. Other firms who made early use of shaft drive included Darracq (21, 27) and Itala (36). The influence of the 1901 Mercedes (17) was very great, not because of any revolutionary features but because it combined such modern characteristics as mechanically-operated inlet valves, magneto ignition, gate-type gearchange and honeycomb radiator, with reliability and a low centre of gravity which made it safer as well as more attractive in appearance than most of its contemporaries. Other manufacturers such as Fiat were quick to follow the Mercedes pattern, particularly after the German firm's success in the 1903 Gordon Bennett Race, and the typical racing car of 1904–6 took on a very different appearance from the high, short-wheelbase machines which were familiar at the turn of the century.

Up to 1903 the main event each year

was the town-to-town race organized by the Automobile Club de France, but in 1902 there took place in Belgium an event whose importance was probably not fully realized at the time. This was the Circuit des Ardennes, in which several laps of a closed circuit were covered in place of the point-to-point system of all previous motor races. There were no neutralized sections as in the town-to-town events, and the 53-mile circuit had simply to be covered six times with no stops except for refuelling and whatever repairs might be necessary. Seventy-five cars took part in the first Circuit des Ardennes, and this meant far more passing, with the inevitable dust problem, than there had been in the open road races. The spectators were happy, however, for they could see their favourite drivers not once but six times. With the abandonment of open-road racing after the disastrous, accident-filled Paris–Madrid race of 1903, circuit racing became the rule, as it has remained ever since.

Apart from the Circuit des Ardennes, which was continued with slight variations in length until 1907, the leading European race was for the Gordon Bennett Cup. This was presented by an American, James Gordon Bennett, who was the proprietor of the *New York Herald* and was otherwise famous as the man who dispatched H. M. Stanley in search of Dr Livingstone. The Cup was to be awarded to national teams rather than individual drivers or makes, and only three cars were allowed to represent each country. An additional stipulation was that all parts of the cars had to be made in the country which was entering them. This did not, however,

apply to the car's design, and Alexandre Darracq took advantage of this in 1904 to enter cars of Darracq design made in Scotland and in Germany as well as native French-made cars (27). The first Gordon Bennett Race was run in June 1900 over a 353-mile course from Paris to Lyons, and attracted only five entries. In 1901 it was combined with Paris–Berlin and in 1902 with Paris–Vienna, the latter event giving Great Britain her first international motor racing victory for S. F. Edge's 40-h.p. Napier (11). The winning country had the privilege (or burden) of organizing the following year's race, and as the British government has always opposed racing on public roads, the 1903 Gordon Bennett Race was held in Ireland and won by Jenatzy's 60-h.p. Mercedes (17). By 1904 so many French manufacturers wanted to enter the Gordon Bennett that the Automobile Club de France had to organize an eliminating trial to choose three competitors from the twenty-nine French cars which aspired to Gordon Bennett honours. These trials, held in 1904 at Mazagran near the Belgian frontier, and in 1905 on the Gordon Bennett circuit itself in the Auvergne, were major events in themselves. British Eliminating Trials were held in 1904 and 1905 in the Isle of Man, though in America Eliminating Trials were held in 1903 only, owing to insufficient starters. Inevitably many manufacturers never got beyond the trials, and their annoyance with this system led to the end of the Gordon Bennett Races after 1905. The first fifteen makes in the 1905 French Eliminating Trials were invited to take part in a new race in 1906 to be known as the Grand Prix de l'Automobile Club de France, and foreign entries were also welcomed. In fact the first Grand Prix was a largely French affair, the only foreign entries coming from Italy (Fiat and Itala) and Germany (Mercedes). It was held on a 103·18-km. circuit outside Le Mans, the first of many associations with motor sport that this town was to have. In order to give the race a standing above any rivals such as the Circuit des Ardennes or the Sicilian Targa Florio, it was run over twelve laps (1238 km.; 769 miles), the racing being spread over two days. The only 'formula' with which the cars had to conform was a maximum weight limit of 1000 kg. Detachable rims were permitted, although only three manufacturers took advantage of this: Renault, Fiat and Clément-Bayard. This was undoubtedly one of the factors which contributed to Renault's victory, for the rough roads were punishing to primitive tires, and tire changing caused more delay to competitors than any other single factor. It was also remarked that more consideration was shown for the mechanic's comfort on the Renault than on other cars, thus enabling him to perform his tasks better.

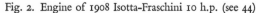

Fig. 2. Engine of 1908 Isotta-Fraschini 10 h.p. (see 44)

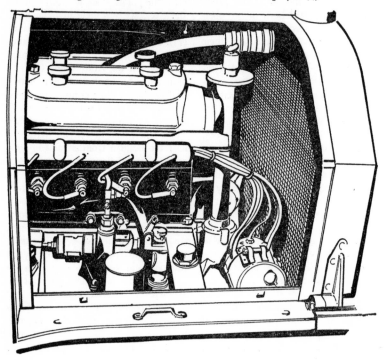

The 1907 Grand Prix was a one-day event held on a 770-km. (477-mile) circuit near Dieppe. In an attempt to bring racing car design more into line with that of the touring car, the weight limit was abolished, and a fuel consumption restriction of 30 litres per 100 km. (9·41 miles per gallon) imposed instead. This did not result in any reduction in average size of engine, and indeed the winning Fiat (29), at 15268 cc., was nearly three litres larger than the 1906 Renault. Design was rather more varied, some unusual cars including three straight-eights (the Swiss Dufaux (30), the French Porthos, and the British Weigel), as well as Walter Christie's extraordinary 19·9-litre front wheel drive vee-four machine (28) which had the largest engine of any

car that has ever competed in a Grand Prix. At this date American designs tended to be more eccentric than European, and a fascinating variety of unusual machines turned up for the eliminating trials for the Vanderbilt Cup Races. These were America's equivalent of the Gordon Bennett Races, and were for national teams of up to five cars each. The Cup was presented by William K. Vanderbilt jun., a keen sportsman and driver of no mean ability. In 1904-6 and 1908-10 the races were held on Long Island, originally close to New York, and later further out in the country. In addition to the stipulation that every part of the car had to be made in the country entering it, there was a weight limit of 2204 lb. Among the entrants for Vanderbilt Cup

Fig. 3. Engine of 1910 Lion-Peugeot VX-5 Coupe des Voiturettes car (see 46)

honours in the period 1904 to 1908 were a steam car from White, an air-cooled straight-eight Franklin, a horizontal twelve cylinder Maxwell and, of course, various manifestations of front wheel drive Christie. However, as usual, eccentricity did not pay off, and the first three Vanderbilt Cup Races went to relatively conventional Panhard and Darracq (27) cars, and the fourth to an equally conventional Locomobile (25).

The 1908 Grand Prix regulations restricted piston area to 117 sq. in., which meant a maximum bore of 155 mm. for four-cylinder engines and 127 mm. for six-cylinder engines. This resulted in slightly smaller capacities in some cases, but other firms simply lengthened the stroke, on which there was no restriction, and the effect on design was not great. Overhead inlet valves were seen on some cars, including Mercedes (37) and the American Locomobile (25), while Clément-Bayard (23) introduced an overhead camshaft on their 1908 Grand Prix cars. Victory went to Lautenschlager's Mercedes, with two other German cars, the Benzes of Hémery and Hanriot, in second and third places. French manufacturers were so disgusted that they resolved to have nothing more to do with Grand Prix racing. Nearly all the firms who had taken part in the 1908 Grand Prix signed an agreement that they would not race in 1909, and the A.C.F. had no alternative but to cancel the Grand Prix they had planned, which would have taken place on a new circuit in Anjou.

Meanwhile there had been many

Fig. 4. Engine of 1912 Peugeot Grand Prix car (see 65)

interesting developments in the world of *voiturette* racing. This had lapsed temporarily after the demise of the town-to-town races in 1903, as the Gordon Bennett Races naturally attracted the more powerful cars. However, light cars themselves were coming on to the roads in increasing numbers, and in 1905 the French magazine *l'Auto* offered a cup for cars of not more than 400 kg. weight and of under 1-litre capacity. The latter restriction was revolutionary, for a weight restriction merely meant that constructors tried to squeeze as large an engine into as flimsy and light a chassis as they dared, but a capacity restriction as low as 1 litre would bring forth a new kind of racing car. The first Coupe de *l'Auto* was a six-day trial with a speed event at the conclusion, and attracted *voiturettes*, mostly with single-cylinder engines, from De Dion-Bouton (43), Vulpès, Lacoste et Battmann, Gladiator, and several other firms whose names had not been familiar in racing before. Unfortunately some anti-motoring fanatic sprinkled part of the route with nails, and the resulting delay to some of the competitors so confused the results that the A.C.F. cancelled the whole competition, and forbade the winners from advertising their successes on pain of a heavy fine. From 1906 to 1910, however, *voiturette* racing flourished, and in addition to the Coupe de *l'Auto* several other light car events were organized, in France, Sicily, and Spain.

It should be pointed out that *l'Auto* presented a cup each year from 1905 to 1913, the races from 1905 to 1910 inclusive being alternatively known as the Coupe des Voiturettes, while the 1911 event was also called the Coupe des Voitures Légères, being for cars of up to 3 litres' capacity. In 1912 and 1913 there was no alternative name. The races grew rapidly in popularity, and for the 1907 event there were no fewer than sixty-seven entries. The formulae imposed a limitation on the cylinder bore which varied from year to year, but except in 1909 no restrictions were made on the stroke. This resulted in extreme stroke/bore ratios, culminating in the 1910 Lion-Peugeot VX5 (46) with dimensions of 80 × 280 mm., and a bonnet so high that driver and mechanic had to peer round it. For a short time these cars were very successful, but it was not a design trend that had any long-term future, largely because of the limit set on engine speed by the high piston speed of the long-stroke engine. The other type of light car developed by the *voiturette* races, although less successful in actual competition, was much more important historically. This was the small four-cylinder machine, with efficient, high-revving, overhead camshaft engine, typified by the Isotta Fraschini (44), Martini (39), and Bugatti (51). These set the pattern for the ideal light car for many years to come, and must have been delightful cars to own, although comparatively few were sold.

While *voiturette* racing flourished, the French manufacturers continued their refusal to enter for a Grand Prix through 1910 and 1911. In the latter year a Grand Prix of a sort was organized, which has caused much confusion among historians. This was organized by l'Automobile Club de l'Ouest based at Le Mans, and they called it the Grand Prix de France, as opposed to the Grand Prix de l'ACF which was the main

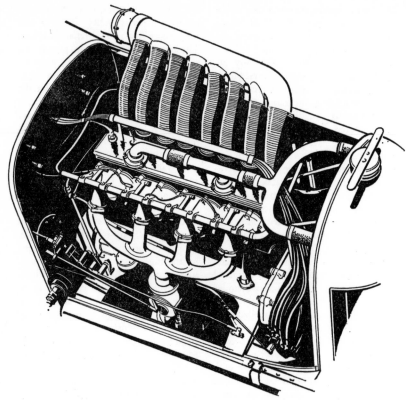

Fig. 5. Engine of 1913 Delage Grand Prix car (see 69)

event organized by the Automobile Club de France in Paris. Unfortunately both events have been translated into English as 'French Grand Prix', and the confusion is not helped by the fact that the ACF revived their own event in 1912, so that in 1912 and 1913 both races were held. The Grand Prix de France was never a very important event, as the big manufacturers refused to build cars for it, so the field was made up of lesser-known cars such as Rolland-

Pilain (54) and ancient cars such as Duray's 1906 Lorraine-Dietrich and Fournier's 1907 Corre-La Licorne. The 1911 race was chiefly notable for the performance of Friderich's little Bugatti, which slipped into second place behind a Fiat (66) of nearly seven times the capacity.

Spurred by the activities of the Automobile Club de l'Ouest, the ACF proposed a Grand Prix of their own in 1912, with no restrictions whatever on

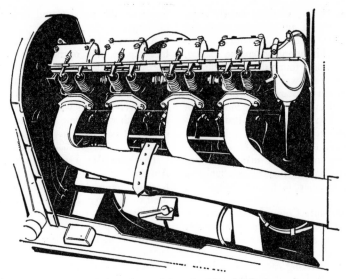

Fig. 6. Engine of 1914 Mercedes Grand Prix (see 77)

design except for a maximum width of 175 cm. (68·5 in.). The minimum number of starters was to be thirty, and to make this a reasonably attainable figure, the Coupe de *l'Auto*, now for 3-litre cars, was to be run concurrently. Entrants in the latter were eligible for the Grand Prix, and as it turned out, a Coupe de *l'Auto* Sunbeam (64) took third place. The race was held on the same circuit at Dieppe which had seen the 1907 and 1908 Grands Prix, and was a two-day event totalling 1540 km. Only fourteen cars started in the Grand Prix, but they were backed up by thirty-three Coupe de *l'Auto* entrants. The race was a struggle between the 'old guard', represented by the enormous chain-driven Fiats (66) and Lorraine-Dietrichs (60), and the new twin overhead camshaft Peugeots (65).

It would not be fair to say that the Peugeots had a sweeping victory, for Bruce-Brown in the Fiat often led Boillot's Peugeot, and although the latter was victorious, his team mates Goux and Zuccarelli both retired. However, the importance of the 1912 Peugeots lay not so much in what they did as what they were. Just as the 1901 Mercedes combined most of the current improvements in a practical and reliable car, so did the Peugeot in 1912. Inclined overhead valves had been seen as early as 1904 on the Pipe (31), and single overhead camshafts were a feature of some of Cattaneo's Isotta Fraschinis (44) from 1905, while the monobloc four-cylinder engine was not unknown either. But the Peugeot design team of the drivers Goux and Zuccarelli and the Swiss draughtsman

Ernest Henry, working largely independently of the factory, combined inclined overhead valves with two camshafts and monobloc engine casting, and also used four valves per cylinder. Engine speed was 2200 r.p.m., which, while not outstanding, was certainly faster than the previous generation of Grand Prix cars. The basic Peugeot layout of inclined overhead valves with twin overhead camshaft was subsequently imitated by many firms including Fiat (75), Nagant (76), Sunbeam (79), Premier (81), and Ballot (83, 87).

The 3-litre Coupe de *l'Auto* cars included some very fine and reliable machines, especially the Sunbeams (64). These and the Vauxhalls (55) were examples of racing cars developed from conventional, standard side-valve touring cars, their engines steadily developed over a period of several years by racing and testing at Brooklands Motor Course. The importance of Brooklands to British racing cars cannot be overestimated, for without any road circuits British manufacturers would have had nowhere to test their cars. As it was, Sunbeam, Vauxhall, Straker-Squire (61), Calthorpe (59), and other firms regularly ran their products at the course, covering thousands of miles sometimes in testing and developing engines which would stand up to several hours of continuous high speed. Brooklands experience also led to the development of pointed tails, cowled radiators, and other streamlining aids which found their way on to the circuit racing machinery. The first Peugeot to have a pointed tail was the 1912 Grand Prix model as raced by Goux at Brooklands, and these tails were not found on the actual Grand Prix cars until 1914.

America's brick-surface track at Indianapolis was opened two years later than Brooklands, in 1909, and the annual 500 Miles Race was first held in 1911. However, the Indianapolis track was never used so widely as Brooklands, either for racing or testing, and could not be said to have had such an important effect on racing car design.

The 1913 Grand Prix was run at Amiens over a 917-km. course, and the formula involved a fuel consumption limit of 14 m.p.g. Because of this, fuel tanks had to be exposed, which eliminated any possibility of streamlined tails that year. The race saw the appearance of the interesting Delage (69) with horizontal valves and five-speed gearbox, but Guyot's accident robbed the marque of the good chance it had of victory. The Peugeots, however, were extremely successful in both the Grand Prix and the Coupe de *l'Auto*, which was a separate race in 1913. The Grand Prix saw the last side-valve cars to compete in this class of racing, Mathis (56), Excelsior (63), and Schneider (68). Other interesting developments of the year were the first appearance of sleeve-valve engines in racing on the 1913 Indianapolis Mercedes, and the end of chain drive, also on a Mercedes, which ran in the Grand Prix de France. The Amiens Grand Prix was the first to be run in a clockwise direction, which afterwards became standardized for all Grand Prix events.

The day after the 1913 Grand Prix there was held on the same course a race for cyclecars, the new breed of light cars often using two-cylinder engines and belt or chain drive. There was a capacity limit of 1100 cc., and the race attracted many makes which had not previously been seen on the race track. Among these were the Violet-Bogey (73), the Duo, the Super, and the extraordinary Bédélia, which was steered from the rear seat, and which won the Amiens event. Another Cyclecar Grand Prix was held three weeks later, in conjunction with the Grand Prix de France at Le Mans, and was won by a Ronteix, with a Violet-Bogey in second place.

There was only one major European race in 1914, the Grand Prix, as the Coupe de l'*Auto* was cancelled because of the outbreak of war. The Grand Prix was run over a 752-km. (466-mile) triangular course south of Lyons. The entries showed a further spread of double overhead camshafts among such makes as Fiat and Nagant, and also the first appearance of four-wheel brakes, on Fiat (75), Delage (69), Peugeot (65), and Piccard-Pictet (74). The race was dominated by the heroic struggle between Georges Boillot in a Peugeot against the might of Mercedes. The significance of the latter lay not so much in its design, which was not the most modern in the race (it had only a single

Fig. 7. Engine of 1920 Monroe-Frontenac (see 86)

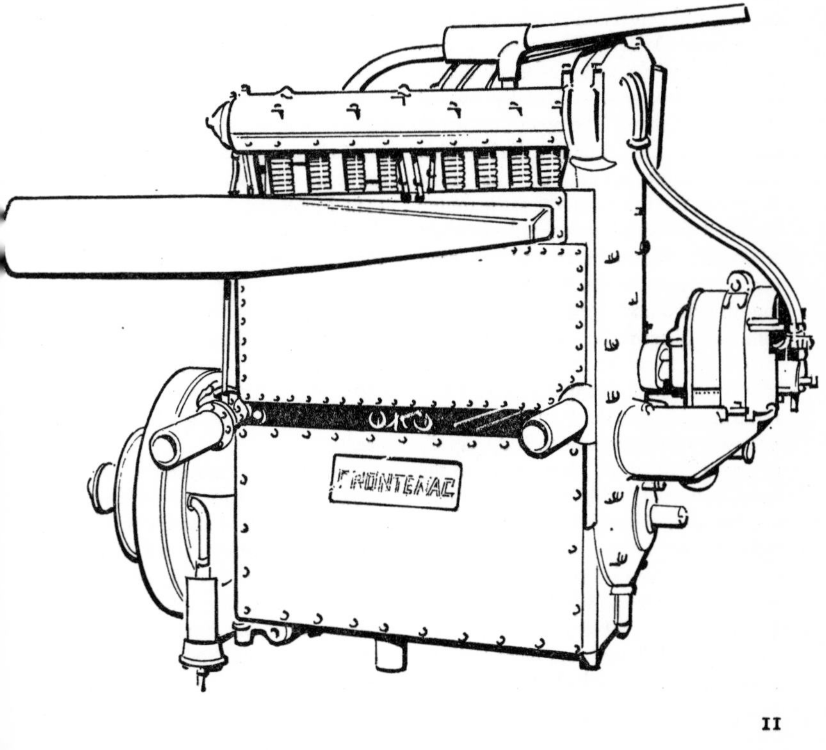

camshaft and two-wheel brakes), but in the superb organization of the team. This included a careful study of the course and provision of a wide choice of alternative gear ratios, and also a definite use of tactics in the race, when Sailer was sent out to drive as fast as he could in order to lure the Peugeot opposition to do the same and break its cars, while the other members of the team hung back. With five cars in the team, Sailer's retirement on the sixth lap was no disaster, and he had done his job.

The war naturally brought all European racing to a stop, and seriously affected the quality and interest of American racing, as many of the leading cars and drivers on American tracks came from Europe. A number of cars were built to the order of the Indianapolis Speedway, who actually owned and entered them. The most famous of these were the Premiers (81) which were straight copies of the 1914 Peugeots, but others on the same theme included the single overhead camshaft Maxwells. Wood board tracks spread across America, no less than seven opening in 1915 and 1916, including the famous Sheepshead Bay track at Brooklyn, New York. The aftermath of war prevented European racing from restarting immediately, and so the first post-war cars were sent to Indianapolis to prove their paces. These included the 1919 Ballot (83) which effectively, if not literally, pioneered the use of eight cylinders in line. This principle appeared on Grand Prix cars in 1921, when Duesenberg (88), Sunbeam (89), Ballot (87), and Fiat (90) all had straight-eight engines. These cars were built to a 3-litre formula which ran for two years, 1920 and 1921. The Coupe de l'Auto was not revived, but for the smaller cars there were *voiturette* races, to a 1400 cc. formula in 1920 and 1500 cc. in 1921. High-tension magneto ignition had been universal from about 1908 onwards, but the 1920 Monroe-Frontenac (86) used a Delco coil in the Indianapolis race, and other makers such as Duesenberg (88) and Sunbeam (89) followed suit. The 1921 Grand Prix cars showed other interesting developments, including the first use of mechanical servo-brake operation (Ballot, 87) and of an all roller-bearing crankshaft (Fiat, 90). Almost all the 1921 Grand Prix cars used straight-eight engines, but this was not a trend followed immediately, as the reduction in the formula from three litres to two in 1922 led to a revival of four- and six-cylinder engines. Because of the steady reduction in engine sizes, there were no dramatic gains in maximum speeds, and the 1921 Fiat was no faster than the 1914 Mercedes, both being capable of about 118 m.p.h. Racing car design in 1921 was poised on the edge of new developments even more significant than those mentioned, such as the supercharger. These were to bring about a marked increase in performance, and even more in power-to-weight ratio, during the next three years.

Most of the cars described in this book were built for racing, but motor sport in the period also included a large number of hill-climbs and straight-line sprint meetings. The high point of the latter was the outright flying kilometre record, which has come to be known as the World's Land Speed Record. Competition for this honour has tended to

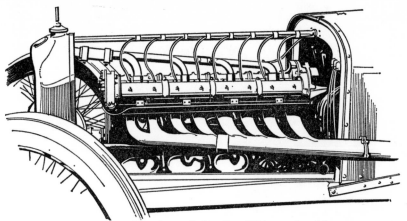

Fig. 8. Engine of 1921 Ballot Grand Prix car (see 87)

come in phases, and the early struggles between Chasseloup-Laubat and Jenatzy (3, 2) have been mirrored by those of Segrave and Campbell in the 1920s and Eyston and Cobb in the 1930s. Mechanical timing was first used at Dourdan, France in 1902 when Henri Fournier drove a 60-h.p. Mors at a speed of 76·6 m.p.h., while a significant landmark was reached in 1904 when Rigolly's Gobron-Brillié (14) achieved a speed of over 100 m.p.h. Up to 1910 the record could be claimed on the basis of a one-way kilometre run, but after that the A.I.A.C.R. (Association Internationale des Automobile Clubs Reconnus) insisted on two runs, the record to consist of the mean of the two. This decision meant that some American runs, made in one direction only, were never recognized as World's Land Speed Records. Many of the early sprint cars, for this is what they were rather than purpose-built machines such as Campbell's Bluebirds and Cobb's Railton-Mobil, were used for hill-climbs and sometimes for racing. The Darracq vee-eight (21) and Blitzen Benz (50) were particularly successful in competitions other than for the outright record; to see the enormous Benz thundering up a narrow, tree-lined road in a German hill-climb must have been an awe-inspiring sight. The last World's Land Speed Record car in this book, the 1920 350-h.p. Sunbeam, was also used for racing and hill-climbs, and was, incidentally, the last car to set up the World's Land Speed Record at Brooklands.

AUTHOR'S NOTES

Any two views of one car are not necessarily to scale; nor are the views of different cars on the same or adjoining pages.

Approximate conversion of cylinder bore and stroke; 25·4 millimetres (mm.) = 1 inch.

Approximate conversion of engine cubic capacity; 16·4 cubic centimetres (c.c.) = 1 cubic inch.

1

Amédée Bollée, 1898. France. Water cooled, two horizontal cylinders. 110×160 mm., 3042 cc. Side valves (automatic inlets). Hot tube ignition. Four forward speeds. Shaft final drive.

LA JAMAIS CONTENTE

2

La Jamais Contente, 1899. France. Electric motor, geared directly to rear axle.

3

Jeantaud, 1899. France. Electric motor. Chain drive.

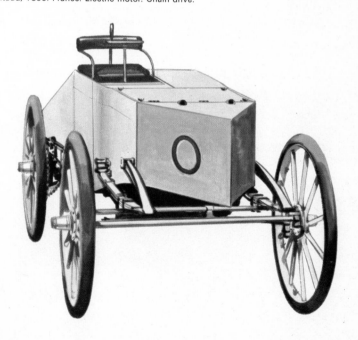

CANNSTATT-DAIMLER

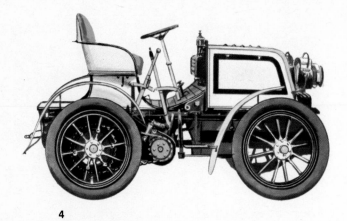

4

Cannstatt-Daimler, 1899. Germany. Water cooled, four vertical cylinders. 106×156 mm., 5507 cc. Side valves (automatic inlets). Low-tension magneto ignition. Four forward speeds. Chain drive.

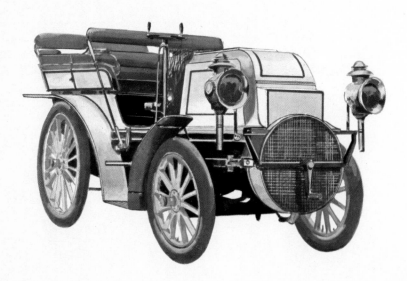

5

Benz, 1900. Germany. Water cooled, two horizontal cylinders. Automatic inlet valves. Four forward speeds. Belt primary drive, chain final drive.

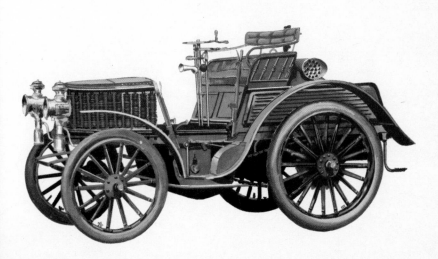

6

Panhard 40 h.p., 1901. France. Water cooled, four vertical cylinders. 130×140 mm., 7433 cc. Side valves (automatic inlets). Coil and battery ignition. Four forward speeds. Chain drive.

7

Mors 60 h.p., 1901. France. Water cooled, four vertical cylinders. 130 × 190 mm., 10,087 cc. Side valves (automatic inlets). Low-tension magneto ignition. Four forward speeds. Chain drive.

RENAULT 16 H.P.

8

Renault 16 h.p., 1902. France. Water cooled, four vertical cylinders. 120×120 mm., 3758 cc. Side valves (automatic inlets). Coil and battery ignition. Three forward speeds. Shaft drive.

9

Spyker, 1902. Netherlands. Water cooled, six vertical cylinders. 120×128 mm., 8676 cc. Side valves in T head. Low-tension magneto ignition. Six forward speeds (plus two reverse). Shaft drive to front and rear wheels.

PANHARD 70 H.P.

10

Panhard 70 h.p., 1902. France. Water cooled, four vertical cylinders. 160×170 mm., 13,672 cc. Side valves (automatic inlets). Coil and battery ignition. Four forward speeds. Chain drive.

11

Napier, 1902. Great Britain. Water cooled, four vertical cylinders. 127×127 mm., 6435 cc. Side valves (automatic inlets). Coil and accumulator ignition. Three forward speeds. Shaft drive.

SERPOLLET

12

Serpollet, 1902. France. 40 n.h.p. steam engine. Flash generator, automatic feed of water to generator and of oil to burner by donkey engine. Four horizontal cylinders. Shaft drive.

13

Winton, 1903. U.S.A. Water cooled, eight horizontal cylinders. 133·25×152·4 mm., 17,016 cc. Side valves (automatic inlets). Coil and battery ignition. One forward speed. Shaft drive.

GOBRON-BRILLIE

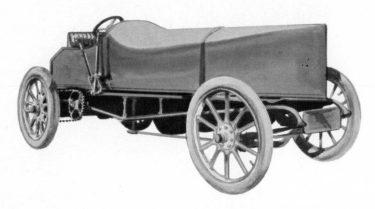

14

Gobron-Brillié, 1903. France. Water cooled, four vertical cylinders (double piston). 140 × 220 mm., 13,547 cc. Side valves in L head. High-tension magneto ignition. Four forward speeds. Chain drive.

15

De Dietrich, 1903. France. Water cooled, four vertical cylinders. 150 × 150 mm., 9896 cc. Side valves in T head (automatic inlets). Low-tension magneto ignition. Three forward speeds. Chain drive.

DE DION BOUTON

16

De Dion Bouton, 1903. France. Water cooled, four vertical cylinders. 90×120 mm., 3054 cc. Side valves. Coil and battery ignition. Three forward speeds. Shaft drive.

17

Mercedes, 1903. Germany. Water cooled, four vertical cylinders. 140×150 mm., 9236 cc. Inlet over exhaust valves. Low-tension magneto ignition. Four forward speeds. Chain drive.

NAPIER

18

Napier, 1904. Great Britain. Water cooled, six vertical cylinders. 158·75 × 127 mm., 15,083 cc. Side valves in L head. Coil and battery ignition. Two forward speeds. shaft drive.

19

Richard-Brasier, 1904 and 1905. France. Water cooled, four vertical cylinders. 150×140 mm., 9896 cc. (1905: 160×140 mm., 11,259 cc.). Side valves in T head. Low-tension magneto ignition. Three forward speeds. Chain drive.

WOLSELEY

20

Wolseley, 1905. Great Britain. Water cooled, four horizontal cylinders. 152·4 ×
165·1 mm., 11,896 cc. Overhead valves. Coil and battery ignition. Four forward
speeds. Chain drive.

DARRACQ

21

Darracq, 1905. France. Water cooled, eight V-formation cylinders. 160×140 mm., 22,518 cc. Overhead valves. Low-tension magneto ignition. Two forward speeds. Shaft drive.

STANLEY

22

Stanley, 1906. U.S.A. Steam engine, two horizontal cylinders. 30-inch, 1,000 p.s.i. boiler. Direct drive.

23

Clément-Bayard, 1906. France. Water cooled, four vertical cylinders. 160×160 mm., 12,868 cc. Side valves. High-tension magneto ignition. Four forward speeds. Shaft drive.

24

Hotchkiss, 1906. France. Water cooled, four vertical cylinders. 180×160 mm., 16,286 cc. Side valves. High-tension magneto ignition. Four forward speeds. Shaft drive.

25

Locomobile, 1906. U.S.A. Water cooled, four vertical cylinders. 184·14×158·7 mm., 16,000 cc. Inlet over exhaust valves. Low-tension magneto ignition. Three forward speeds. Chain drive.

26

Renault, 1906. France. Water cooled, four vertical cylinders. 166×150 mm., 12,975 cc. Side valves in L head. High-tension magneto ignition. Three forward speeds. Shaft drive.

27

Darracq, 1906. France. Water cooled, four vertical cylinders. 170×140 mm., 12,711 cc. Side valves. Low-tension magneto ignition. Three forward speeds. Shaft drive.

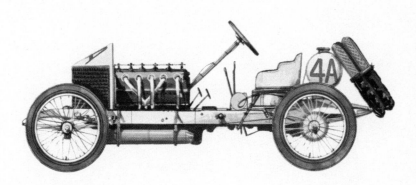

CHRISTIE

28

Christie, 1907. U.S.A. Water cooled, four V-formation cylinders. 185×185 mm., 19,891 cc. Coil and battery ignition. Two forward speeds. Direct drive to front wheels.

29

Fiat, 1907. Italy. Water cooled, four vertical cylinders. 180×150 mm., 15,268 cc.
Side valves in T head. Low-tension magneto ignition. Four forward speeds.
Chain drive.

DUFAUX

30

Dufaux, 1907. Switzerland. Water cooled, eight vertical cylinders. 125 × 130 mm., 12,761 cc. Side valves. High-tension magneto ignition. Four forward speeds. Chain drive.

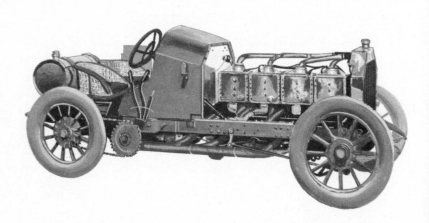

31

Pipe, 1907. Belgium. Water cooled, four vertical cylinders. 140×128 mm.,
7940 cc. Inclined overhead valves. High-tension magneto ignition. Four forward
speeds. Chain drive.

BERLIET

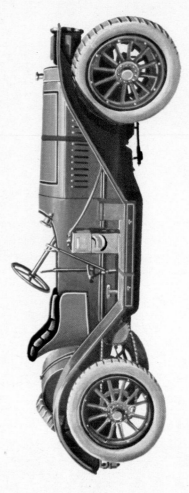

32

Berliet, 1907. France. Water cooled, four vertical cylinders, 127 × 127 mm., 6424 cc. Side valves. High-tension magneto ignition. Four forward speeds. Chain drive.

MARTINI

33

Martini, 1907. Switzerland. Water
cooled, four vertical cylinders. 134 ×
140 mm., 7833 cc. Side valves. High-
tension magneto ignition. Three forward speeds. Chain drive.

MINERVA

34

Minerva, 1907. Belgium. Water cooled, four vertical cylinders, 145×120 mm., 7910 cc. Inlet over exhaust valves. High-tension magneto ignition. Three forward speeds. Chain drive.

35

Napier, 1908. Great Britain. Water cooled, six vertical cylinders. 127 × 152·4 mm.,
11,580 cc. Inlet over exhaust valves. High-tension magneto ignition. Three
forward speeds. Shaft drive.

ITALA

36

Itala, 1908. Italy. Water cooled, four vertical cylinders. 155×160 mm., 12,060 cc. Side valves. Low-tension magneto ignition. Four forward speeds. Shaft drive.

37

Mercedes, 1908. Germany. Water cooled, four vertical cylinders. 155×170 mm., 12,781 cc. Inlet over exhaust valves. High-tension magneto ignition. Four forward speeds. Chain drive.

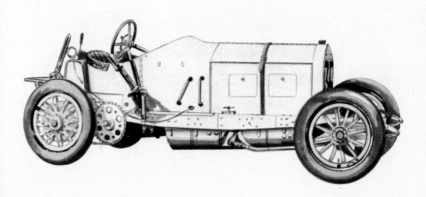

AUSTIN

38

Austin, 1908. Great Britain. Water cooled, six vertical cylinders. 127×127 mm., 9635 cc. Side valves in T head. High-tension magneto ignition. Four forward speeds. Shaft or chain drive.

MARTINI

39

Martini, 1908. Switzerland. Water cooled, four vertical cylinders. 62×90 mm., 1086 cc. Overhead valves operated by overhead camshaft. High-tension magneto ignition. Three forward speeds. Shaft drive.

THOMAS

40

Thomas, 1908. U.S.A. Water cooled, four vertical cylinders. 150×150 mm., 11,321 cc. Side valves in T head. High-tension magneto ignition. Four forward speeds. Chain drive.

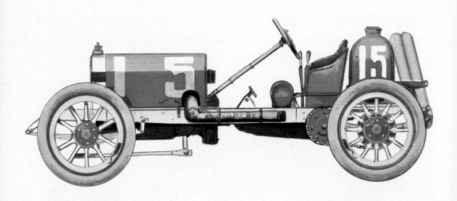

41

Opel, 1908. Germany. Water cooled, four vertical cylinders. 155×160 mm., 12,045 cc. Side valves in L head. High-tension magneto ignition. Four forward speeds. Shaft drive.

HUTTON

42

Hutton, 1908. Great Britain. Water cooled, four vertical cylinders. 101×178 mm., 5760 cc. Side valves. High-tension magneto ignition. Four forward speeds. Shaft drive.

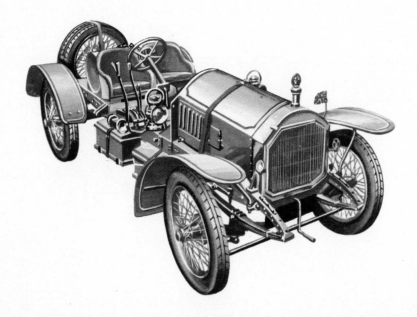

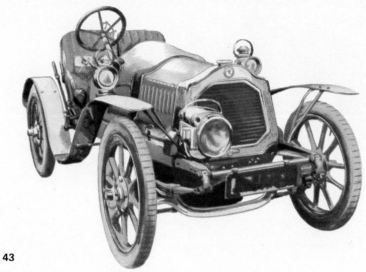

43

De Dion Bouton, 1908.
France. Water cooled, one
vertical cylinder. 100×160
mm., 1260 cc. Side valves.
High-tension magneto ignition. Three forward speeds.
Shaft drive.

ISOTTA FRASCHINI

44

Isotta Fraschini, 1908. Italy. Water cooled, four vertical cylinders. 65×100 mm., 1327 cc. Overhead valves operated by overhead camshaft. High-tension magneto ignition. Four forward speeds. Shaft drive.

VAUXHALL

45

Vauxhall, 1909. Great Britain. Water cooled, four vertical cylinders. 90×120 mm., 3053 cc. Side valves in L head. High-tension magneto ignition. Four forward speeds. Shaft drive.

LION-PEUGEOT

46

Lion-Peugeot, 1910. France. Water cooled, two V-formation cylinders. 80 × 280 mm., 2816 cc. Inlet over exhaust valves. High-tension magneto ignition. Four forward speeds. Chain drive.

47

Hispano-Suiza, 1910. Spain. Water cooled, four vertical cylinders. 65 × 200 mm., 2655 cc. Side valves in T head. High-tension magneto ignition. Three forward speeds. Shaft drive.

SUNBEAM

48

Sunbeam, 1911. Great Britain. Water cooled, four vertical cylinders. 80 × 160 mm., 3215 cc. Overhead valves operated by overhead camshaft. High-tension magneto ignition. Three forward speeds. Shaft drive.

49

Austin, 1911. Great Britain. Water cooled, four vertical cylinders. 89×115 mm.,
2862 cc. Side valves in T head. High-tension magneto ignition. Three forward
speeds. Shaft drive.

BENZ

50

Benz, 1911. Germany. Water cooled, four vertical cylinders. 185×200 mm., 21,504 cc. Side valves in T head. High-tension magneto ignition. Four forward speeds. Chain drive.

51

Bugatti, 1911. Germany. Water cooled, four vertical cylinders. 66×100 mm., 1368 cc. Overhead valves operated by overhead camshaft. High-tension magneto ignition. Four forward speeds. Shaft drive.

DELAGE

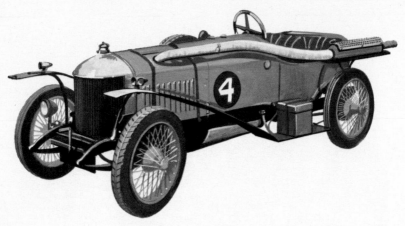

52

Delage, 1911. France. Water cooled, four vertical cylinders, 80×149 mm., 2996 cc. horizontal valves. High-tension magneto ignition. Five forward speeds. Shaft drive.

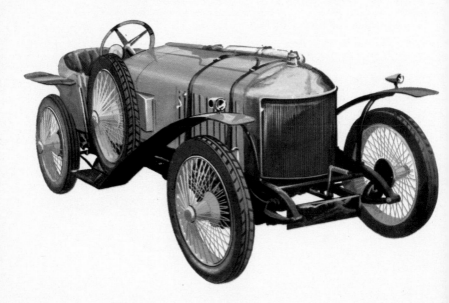

53

Grégoire, 1912. France. Water cooled, four vertical cylinders, 80×149 mm., 2996 cc. Side valves in T head. Dual high-tension magneto ignition. Six forward speeds. Shaft drive.

ROLLAND-PILAIN

54

Rolland-Pilain, 1912. France. Water cooled, four vertical cylinders. 110×165 mm., 6272 cc. Overhead valves operated by overhead camshaft. High-tension magneto ignition. Four forward speeds. Chain drive.

55

Vauxhall, 1912. Great Britain. Water cooled, four vertical cylinders. 90×118 mm., 2991 cc. Side valves in L head. High-tension magneto ignition. Four forward speeds. Shaft drive.

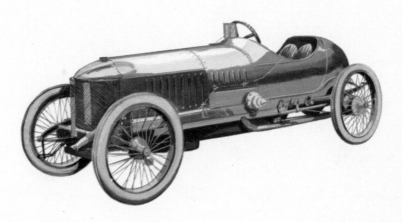

56

Mathis, 1912. Germany. Water cooled, four vertical cylinders. 70×120 mm., 1849 cc. Side valves in L head. High-tension magneto ignition. Four forward speeds. Shaft drive.

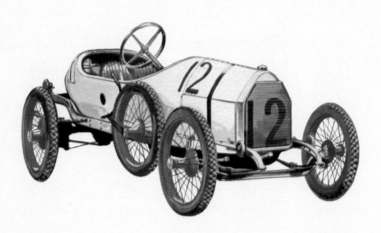

57

Alcyon, 1912. France. Water cooled, four vertical cylinders, 85×132 mm., 2986 cc. Side valves in T head. High-tension magneto ignition. Four forward speeds. Shaft drive.

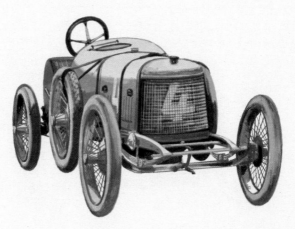

58

Côte, 1912. France. Water cooled, four vertical cylinders. 85×132 mm., 2986 cc. Valveless (two-stroke). High-tension magneto ignition. Four forward speeds. Shaft drive.

59

Calthorpe, 1912. Great Britain. Water cooled, four vertical cylinders. 80×149 mm., 2996 cc. Side valves in L head. High-tension magneto ignition. Four forward speeds. Shaft drive.

LORRAINE-DIETRICH

60

Lorraine-Dietrich, 1912. France. Water cooled, four vertical cylinders. 155 × 200 mm., 15,095 cc. Overhead valves. Dual high-tension magneto ignition. Four forward speeds. Chain drive.

61

Straker-Squire, 1912. Great Britain. Water cooled, four vertical cylinders. 87×120 mm., 2853 cc. Inlet over exhaust valves. High-tension magneto ignition. Four forward speeds. Shaft drive.

SIZAIRE-NAUDIN

62

Sizaire-Naudin, 1912. France. Water cooled, four vertical cylinders. 78×156 mm., 2962 cc. Side valves in T head. High-tension magneto ignition. Four forward speeds. Shaft drive.

63

Excelsior, 1912. Belgium. Water cooled, six vertical cylinders. 110×160 mm., 9138 cc. Side valves in L head. High-tension magneto ignition. Five forward speeds. Shaft drive.

SUNBEAM

64

Sunbeam, 1912. Great Britain. Water cooled, four vertical cylinders. 80×149 mm., 2996 cc. Side valves in L head. High-tension magneto ignition. Four forward speeds. Shaft drive.

65

Peugeot, 1912. France. Water cooled, four vertical cylinders. 110×200 mm., 7603 cc. Overhead valves operated by two overhead camshafts. High-tension magneto ignition. Four forward speeds. Shaft drive.

FIAT

66

Fiat, 1912. Italy. Water cooled, four vertical cylinders. 150×200 mm., 14,137 cc.
Overhead valves. High-tension magneto ignition. Four forward speeds. Chain
drive.

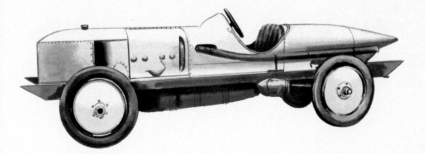

67

Talbot, 1913. Great Britain. Water cooled, four vertical cylinders. 101·5 × 140 mm., 4531 cc. Side valves in L head. High-tension magneto ignition. Four forward speeds. Shaft drive.

68

Schneider, 1913. France. Water cooled, four vertical cylinders. 96 × 190 mm., 5501 cc. Side valves in L head. High-tension magneto ignition. Four forward speeds. Shaft drive.

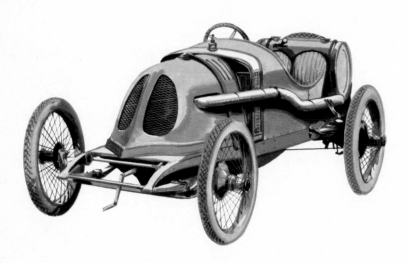

DELAGE

69

Delage, 1913. France. Water cooled, four vertical cylinders. 110×185 mm., 7032 cc. Horizontal valves in head. High-tension magneto ignition. Five forward speeds. Shaft drive.

ITALA

70

Itala, 1913. Italy. Water cooled, four vertical cylinders. 125 × 170 mm., 8325 cc.
Rotary valves. High-tension magneto ignition. Four forward speeds. Shaft drive.

DUESENBERG

71

Duesenberg, 1914. U.S.A. Water cooled, four vertical cylinders. 111×152 mm., 5920 cc. Horizontal overhead valves. High-tension magneto ignition. Four forward speeds. Shaft drive.

A.L.F.A., ALFA ROMEO

72

A.L.F.A., 1914; Alfa Romeo, 1920. Italy. *Top:* water cooled, four vertical cylinders. 100×130 mm., 4084 cc. Side valves in L head. High tension magneto ignition. Four forward speeds. Shaft drive. *Bottom:* water cooled, four vertical cylinders. 102×130 mm., 4250 cc. Side valves in L head. High-tension magneto ignition. Four forward speeds. Shaft drive.

73

Violet-Bogey, 1913. France. Water cooled, four vertical cylinders. 73×130 mm., 1088 cc. Inlet over exhaust valves. High-tension magneto ignition. Friction transmission. Chain drive.

PICCARD-PICTET

74

Piccard-Pictet, 1914. Switzerland. Water cooled, four vertical cylinders. 97×150 mm., 4434 cc. Single sleeve valves. High-tension magneto ignition. Four forward speeds. Shaft drive.

75

Fiat, 1914. Italy. Water cooled, four vertical cylinders. 100×143 mm., 4493 cc.
Overhead valves operated by two overhead camshafts. High-tension magneto
ignition. Four forward speeds. Shaft drive.

NAGANT

76

Nagant, 1914. Belgium. Water cooled, four vertical cylinders. 94·5×158 mm., 4433 cc. Overhead valves operated by two overhead camshafts. High-tension magneto ignition. Five forward speeds. Shaft drive.

77

Mercedes, 1914. Germany. Water cooled, four vertical cylinders. 93×165 mm., 4483 cc. Overhead valves operated by single overhead camshaft. Dual high-tension magneto ignition. Four forward speeds. Shaft drive.

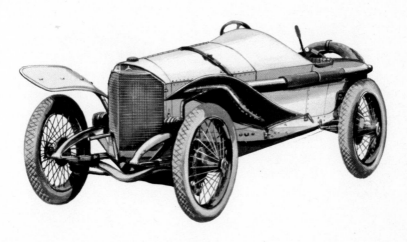

78

Opel, 1914. Germany. Water cooled, four vertical cylinders. 94×160 mm., 4441 cc. Overhead valves operated by single overhead camshaft. High-tension magneto ignition. Four forward speeds. Shaft drive.

SUNBEAM

79

Sunbeam, 1914. Great Britain. Water cooled, four vertical cylinders. 81·5×156 mm., 3296 cc. Overhead valves operated by two overhead camshafts. High-tension magneto ignition. Four forward speeds. Shaft drive.

STUTZ

80

Stutz, 1915. U.S.A. Water cooled, four vertical cylinders. 97 × 165 mm., 4916 cc. Overhead valves operated by single overhead camshaft. High-tension magneto ignition. Three forward speeds. Shaft drive.

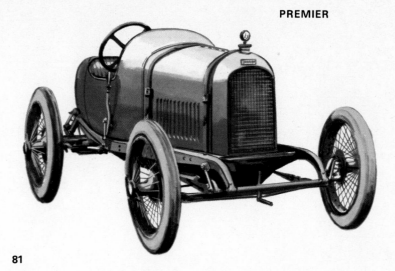

81

Premier, 1916. U.S.A. Water cooled, four vertical cylinders. 93×168 mm., 4500 cc. Overhead valves operated by two overhead camshafts. High-tension magneto ignition. Four forward speeds. Shaft drive.

STRAKER-SQUIRE

82

Straker-Squire, 1918. Great Britain. Water cooled, six vertical cylinders. 80×130 mm., 3915 cc. Overhead valves operated by single overhead camshaft. High-tension magneto ignition. Four forward speeds. Shaft drive.

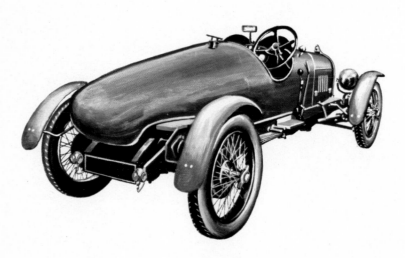

83

Ballot, 1919. France. Water cooled, eight vertical cylinders. 74×140 mm.,
4820 cc. Overhead valves operated by two overhead camshafts. High-tension
magneto ignition. Four forward speeds. Shaft drive.

SUNBEAM

84

Sunbeam, 1920. Great Britain. Water cooled, twelve V-formation cylinders.
120×135 mm., 18,322 cc. Overhead valves operated by two overhead camshafts (one to each bank of cylinders). Dual high-tension magneto ignition.
Four forward speeds. Shaft drive.

85

Peugeot, 1920. France. Water cooled, four vertical cylinders. 80×149 mm., 2996 cc. Overhead valves operated by three overhead camshafts. High-tension magneto ignition. Four forward speeds. Shaft drive.

86

Frontenac, 1921; Monroe-Frontenac, 1920. U.S.A. *Top*: water cooled, eight vertical cylinders. 67×107 mm., 2980 cc. Overhead valves operated by two overhead camshafts. Coil ignition. Three forward speeds. Shaft drive. *Bottom*: water cooled, four vertical cylinders. 79×152 mm., 2980 cc. Overhead valves operated by two overhead camshafts. Coil ignition. Three forward speeds. Shaft drive.

87

Ballot, 1921. France. Water cooled, eight vertical cylinders. 66×112 mm., 2980 cc. Overhead valves operated by two overhead camshafts. High-tension magneto ignition. Four forward speeds. Shaft drive.

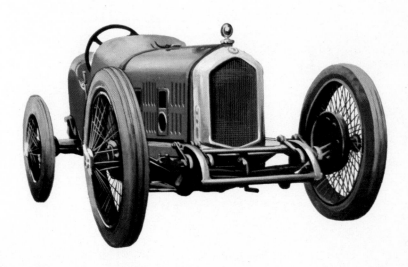

88

Duesenberg, 1921. U.S.A. Water cooled, eight vertical cylinders. 63·5 × 117 mm., 2980 cc. Overhead valves operated by single overhead camshaft. Coil ignition. Three forward speeds. Shaft drive.

89

Sunbeam, 1921. Great Britain. Water cooled, eight vertical cylinders. 65×112 mm., 2974 cc. Overhead valves operated by two overhead camshafts. Coil ignition. Four forward speeds. Shaft drive.

90

Fiat, 1921. Italy. Water cooled, eight vertical cylinders. 65×112 mm., 2974 cc.
Overhead valves operated by two overhead camshafts. High-tension magneto
ignition. Four forward speeds. Shaft drive.

91

Austro-Daimler, 1921. Austria. Water cooled, six vertical cylinders. 74 × 116 mm., 2992 cc. Overhead valves operated by two overhead camshafts. High-tension magneto ignition. Four forward speeds. Shaft drive.

CHITTY-BANG-BANG I

92

Chitty-Bang-Bang I, 1921. Great Britain. Water cooled, six vertical cylinders. 165×180 mm., 23,092 cc. Overhead valves operated by pushrods. High-tension magneto ignition. Four forward speeds. Chain drive.

HORSTMAN

93

Horstman, 1921. Great Britain. Water cooled, four vertical cylinders. 66×109 mm., 1498 cc. Side valves in L head. High-tension magneto ignition. Three forward speeds. Shaft drive.

ASTON MARTIN

94

Aston Martin, 1921. Great Britain. Water cooled, four vertical cylinders.
66·5×107 mm., 1486 cc. Side valves in L head. High-tension magneto ignition.
Three forward speeds. Shaft drive.

95

Talbot-Darracq, 1921. France. Water cooled, four vertical cylinders. 65×112 mm., 1486 cc. Overhead valves operated by two overhead camshafts. Coil ignition. Four forward speeds. Shaft drive.

A.C.

96

A.C., 1921. Great Britain. Water cooled, four vertical cylinders. 69×100 mm., 1496 cc. Overhead valves operated by single overhead camshaft. High-tension magneto ignition. Four forward speeds. Shaft drive.

1 AMÉDÉE BOLLÉE, 1898, France

Amédée Bollée *fils* was the son of Amédée Bollée *père* who had built some steam carriages of advanced design between 1873 and 1885. The younger Bollée began manufacture of gasoline-engined cars in 1896, turning out a *vis-à-vis* with a horizontal two-cylinder engine, hot-tube ignition, and belt drive. One of these competed in the Paris–Marseilles–Paris race of 1896 with its designer at the wheel, but crashed into a tree which had fallen into its path. For the 1898 Paris–Amsterdam–Paris race Amédée Bollée prepared four cars which were probably the first machines in the world intentionally designed for racing. They had torpedo-shaped aluminium bodies and two-cylinder horizontal engines rated at 8 h.p. Drive was by belts to the gears, which were at the back of the car, and thence by two longitudinal shafts to each rear wheel, which was driven by a bevel gear. Four of these cars started in the Paris–Amsterdam race, driven by Bollée himself, Giraud, Loysel, and Vinet, while Baron de Turckheim drove a smaller 6-h.p. car. At the end of the outward stage three of the cars occupied the first three places, but a series of accidents on the return leg allowed the Panhards to get ahead, and the best placed Bollée was Giraud's in third position. Later in 1898 Loysel won the 182-mile Bordeaux–Biarritz race, while Giraud made fastest time of the day for gasoline-engined cars at the Chanteloup hill-climb. Bollée received a number of orders for replicas of these

streamlined machines, some of which were built in the de Dietrich factory at Niederbronn in Alsace. One of these, made to the order of the Comte de Paiva, had a body by Muhlbacher with the advanced feature of a sloping windshield, not generally seen on cars until the 1920s.

In 1899 Bollée built a still more revolutionary racing car with 20-h.p. horizontal four-cylinder engine whose cylinders were cast *en bloc*. The chassis was underslung below the rear axle, giving a very low appearance to the car. It was very fast, with a claimed maximum speed of 60 m.p.h., but unreliable, and in the major race of 1899, the Tour de France, its best placing was Castelnau's fifth. Amédée Bollée made no more racing cars, but turned out high-quality touring cars in small numbers until the outbreak of war in 1914.

2 LA JAMAIS CONTENTE, 1899, France

Camille Jenatzy was a Belgian who trained as a civil engineer but set up in business in Paris as a manufacturer of electric cars, cabs, and delivery vans. When the Comte de Chasseloup-Laubat established a record for the one-way kilometre in December 1898 (3) Jenatzy was spurred to challenge this figure, and built an electric car with which, in January 1899, he achieved a speed of 41·42 m.p.h. Chasseloup-Laubat replied with 43·69 m.p.h., and for several months the French Count and the Belgian engineer engaged in a ding-dong battle for the record, which changed hands several times. Finally, Jenatzy built a highly streamlined machine which he christened *La Jamais Contente*. It had a cigar-shaped body of quite unbroken lines from front to rear and pointed at each end, large section pneumatic tires specially made by Michelin, and tiller steering. Electric motors were geared directly to the rear axle. In April 1899 Jenatzy reached a speed of 65·75 m.p.h. with this machine. Chasseloup-Laubat, whose record cars had been no more than modified tourers, abandoned the struggle, and the World's Land Speed Record, as it came to be known later, remained with Jenatzy for three years. He subsequently had a distinguished career as a racing driver at the wheel of Mercedes cars, and died as a result of a hunting accident in 1913.

La Jamais Contente survives to the present day, and can be seen in the Musée National de la Voiture et du Tourisme at Compiègne, France.

3 JEANTAUD, 1898–1899, France

Charles Jeantaud was a pioneer manufacturer of electric vehicles in France and entered a large six-seater carriage in the world's first motor race, the 1895 Paris–Bordeaux event. One of his customers was the Comte de Chasseloup-Laubat, who entered a light two-seater car in the speed trials organized by the magazine *La France Automobile* at Achères in December 1898. It was the first meeting at which speeds over a measured distance were recorded by official time-keepers, with the object of

establishing accurately the capabilities of different cars. The competitors had to cover a standing-start kilometre, followed by a flying start. The burst of power over a short distance which was one of the properties of an electric car stood Chasseloup-Laubat in good stead, and he recorded the fastest time of the day, 57 seconds for the flying kilometre, which was equivalent to a speed of 39·24 m.p.h. He was promptly challenged by a Belgian engineer, Camille Jenatzy (2), who brought his electric car to the next Achères meeting in January 1899. As Jenatzy was the challenger he was entitled to the first attempt, reaching a speed of 41·42 m.p.h., but Chasseloup-Laubat replied with 43·69 m.p.h., a time which would have been better still had his motor not burnt out 200 yards from the finish. Jenatzy returned to the contest ten days later, reaching a speed of 50 m.p.h., to which Chasseloup-Laubat replied with 57·6 m.p.h. He was still using a touring model Jeantaud, although after the first run he had fitted a lightweight body with some pretence at streamlining. When Jenatzy produced his specially-built car *La Jamais Contente* (2) Chasseloup-Laubat found that he could not compete, and after Jenatzy had achieved 65·75 m.p.h. in April 1899 the Count withdrew from the contest.

4 CANNSTATT-DAIMLER, 1899, Germany

With Carl Benz, Gottlieb Daimler was a pioneer of motor-car manufacture in Germany. His cars first went into serious production in 1895. They had rear-mounted two-cylinder engines and remained in production until 1900, but were supplemented in 1897 by the Phoenix model with engine at the front and four-speed gear-box in place of the belt transmission of the earlier cars. The car illustrated is the racing version of the Phoenix built in 1899 at the suggestion of Emil Jellinek, Austro-Hungarian Consul at Nice and at that time the chief instigator of sporting activities at Cannstatt. The car had a four-cylinder engine of 5·5 litres' capacity variously rated at 24 or 28 h.p., a honeycomb radiator mounted below the bonnet and between the front wheels, and double-chain final drive. The short wheelbase and high centre of gravity made it one of the most dangerous of early racing cars, and despite a creditable top speed of 45 m.p.h. its sporting career was not distinguished. Jellinek drove one at the Nice Speed Week in March 1899, but did not enter it in the Nice–Castellane–Nice race, and indeed the Phoenix did not appear in any of the major races of 1899. In the Nice–Marseilles race in 1900 Jellinek drove one; both car and driver were entered under the name Mercedes. He finished tenth and last. At the La Turbie hill-climb a few days later Wilhelm Bauer was killed when his Phoenix ran wide at the first corner and crashed into some rocks. This was the end of the car's career and work began, again at Jellinek's suggestion, on a new car which appeared in 1901 as the 35-h.p. Mercedes.

Five of the 24-h.p. Phoenixes were built, one coming to England in the hands of Count Eliot Zborowski. It was later used as a fast road car and then as power for a circular saw on an estate in Wiltshire, until it was bought for restoration in 1954 by Francis Hutton-Stott. In 1969 it was sold to the Daimler-Benz company for exhibition in their museum at Stuttgart. Another crossed the Atlantic into the hands of Mr William K. Vanderbilt, who made the fastest time of the day with it at a hill-climb at Newport, Long Island in 1900.

5 BENZ, 1900, Germany

Karl Benz was fundamentally opposed to racing, so there were no works entries from his company in the early days. Nevertheless, a number of private owners entered their cars in competitions, starting with Emile Roger, the Paris agent, whose car finished fourteenth in the Paris–Rouen Trial of 1894. Hans Thun and Fritz Held drove a Roger-Benz in Paris–Bordeaux–Paris in 1896, finishing fifth, while Roger himself finished eighth. Roger-Benzes also ran in Paris–Marseilles–Paris in 1896 and various other small races up to 1900. The 16-h.p. car of 1900 illustrated was more of a special racer than its predecessors, although it was listed in the firm's catalogue. It had four forward speeds and a maximum speed of 40 m.p.h. In it Fritz Held and Richard Benz won the Berlin–Leipzig race. This was possibly a works entry, as the prize, a gold medal bearing a portrait of the Kaiser, went to the Benz company rather than to Held, who was a leading concessionaire for the make. The belt-driven Benzes were not seen in competitions after 1900, and the name next appeared in 1903 when Marius Barbarou, who was chief engineer of Benz by that time, drove a 40-h.p. shaft-driven car in Paris–Madrid. He finished well down the list.

6 PANHARD 40 h.p., 1901, France

From the beginning of motoring in France the firm of Panhard et Levassor of the Avenue d'Ivry, Paris was one of the most important, and their victory in the world's first motor race, from Paris to Bordeaux in 1895, began a highly successful racing career. By 1901 there were two sizes of Panhard racing cars made, a 12-h.p., 3·3-litre *voiture légère* and the 40-h.p., 7·4-litre *grande voiture* illustrated. This had electric ignition (coil) for the first time, previous Panhard racing cars having relied on the outmoded hot tube ignition. It did not have a particularly successful season, taking second place to the new Mors (7) in the Paris–Bordeaux and Paris–Berlin races, when the drivers were Maurice Farman and Léonce Girardot respectively. The Gordon Bennett Race was run concurrently with the Paris–Bordeaux but attracted very few entries, so Girardot's victory was a hollow one. He was ninth in the race as a whole, and was the only Gordon Bennett competitor to finish at all. Lesser successes for the 40-h.p. Panhard were Maurice Farman's win in the Grand Prix de Pau, and Caltellotti's second place in the Giro d'Italia. The 12-h.p. Panhards which ran in the *voiture légère* category were more successful than their larger brothers, winning their class in both Paris–Bordeaux and Paris–Berlin; in the latter race they occupied the first three places in their class.

The 40-h.p. cars were raced again at the beginning of the 1902 season, their weight reduced by some 300 kg. to bring them within the new 1000-kg.

limit. In the Circuit du Nord alcohol race they finished first and second, doing much better than the new 70-h.p. car (10).

7 MORS 60 h.p., 1901, France

In the early years of motor racing the dominant make was Panhard, but for a brief period of four years, 1900 to 1903, they were strongly challenged by the products of the electrical engineer Emile Mors. The original Mors cars had rear-mounted, two-cylinder engines, followed by vee-fours in 1898, but the following year a line of conventional cars with front-mounted four-cylinder, in-line engines appeared, designed by Henri Brasier (19), and it was on this foundation that Mors' sporting reputation was built. The 24-h.p., 7·3-litre racing Mors of 1900 won the Bordeaux–Perigueux–Bordeaux and Paris–Tououse–Paris races, both times with Alfred Levegh at the wheel. For 1901 the company came up with a larger machine of 60 h.p. and 10·1 litres' capacity. Like its predecessors it had automatic inlet valves and low-tension magneto ignition, four speeds and double-chain drive. This car had a very successful season, winning the two main events of 1901, Paris–Bordeaux and Paris–Berlin. In both races Henri Fournier was the driver. The 1902 racing Mors was rather smaller at 9236 cc., but it was notable for the use of shock absorbers. Mors did not have such a good season, their best placings being second and third (Gabriel and Vanderbilt) in the Circuit des Ardennes, but in 1903 a derivative of the 1902 car, now with mechanically operated inlet valves and a streamlined 'upturned boat' body was leading the gruelling Paris–Madrid race when it was stopped at Bordeaux. Gabriel was the driver and his team mate Salleron was second. Although Mors continued to support major races until 1908, they had no further victories.

8 **RENAULT 16 h.p.**, 1902, France

The cars of Louis Renault were remarkable for the use of shaft drive from the start of production in 1898, Renault being one of the few makers of the time never to have used chain or belt drive. Aster or de Dion engines were employed at first, but in 1902 Renault began to manufacture his own engines for his larger cars. These were designed by M. Viet, who was formerly with de Dion Bouton. For the Paris–Vienna race, Renault entered three 16-h.p. cars in the *voiture légère* category, driven by himself, his brother Marcel, and Louvet, as well as four 8-h.p. cars in the *voiturette* class. Marcel Renault not only took the *voiture légère* class but won the whole race, arriving at Vienna 45 minutes before the first of the large cars, the 40-h.p. Mercedes of Count Eliot Zborowski. Two of the *voiturettes* were second and third behind a Darracq. The *voitures légères* of 1903 had larger 30-h.p. engines of 6·3 litres' capacity and mechanically operated inlet valves, but were of generally similar design to the 1902 cars. It was in one of these that Marcel Renault was killed during the Paris–Madrid race, and when Louis heard the news he withdrew all his cars,

although he himself was leading his class. The name Renault was not prominent again until the Grand Prix of 1906 (26).

9 **SPYKER**, 1902, Netherlands

The Spyker was the best-known Dutch make of car, being made from 1899 to 1925. Although the manufacturer's reputation was built on cars of solid, conventional design, they experimented with many unusual devices, some of which were incorporated on production cars. These included compressed air starters, pneumatic transmissions, worm-driven transverse camshafts and, in 1902, four-wheel drive and braking. The latter features were found on an experimental car, which was also unusual in having a six-cylinder engine a good twelve months before S. F. Edge's six-cylinder Napier was announced. This engine was a 8·7-litre 'T'-head unit developing about 40 b.h.p., although later publicity called it a 60 h.p. In the offside of the gearbox was a differential connecting the two propeller shafts, which ran to offset differentials on front and rear axles. A contracting transmission brake on the front shaft provided braking on the front wheels, while there were conventional drum brakes on the rear wheels. The car was not built for racing, although there were plans to enter it in the 1903 Paris–Madrid and 1904 Gordon Bennett Race. However, components frequently broke on test, and it did not seem up to several hundred miles of racing. It was shown at the 1903 Paris Salon and at the 1904 Crystal Palace Show in London, where it climbed the steps to the main hall, and put in some fast demonstration hill-climbs. It was later rebodied as a four-seater, than as a two-seater again, but with oversize tires and a sharply pointed honeycomb radiator in place of the original gilled tubes. In this form (illustrated) it survives today in the collection of Mr Max Lips of Drunen, Holland.

Jarrott won from Gabriel's 60-h.p. Mors.

The 1903 cars were again considerably modified, with mechanically operated inlet valves, pressed steel frames and radiator shells, while the engine was now of 80 h.p. Pierre de Crawhez won the Circuit des Ardennes, but the best the firm could do in Paris–Madrid was fourth place, again with de Crawhez at the wheel.

10 **PANHARD 70 h.p.**, 1902, France

Panhard's big racing car for 1902 was a logical development of their 1901 40-h.p. car (6), but had a number of innovations including three inlet valves per cylinder and a single transverse front spring in place of the more usual longitudinal ones. There was no sub-frame, the engine being bolted directly to the chassis, which was of armoured-wood construction. Inlet valves were still automatic, as Panhard did not go over to mechanical actuation until 1903 on their Paris–Madrid cars. The 1902 car was 200 kg. lighter than its pre-decessor. René de Knyff drove one in the Circuit du Nord alcohol race, but the car suffered from teething troubles and he finished only seventh. No fewer than eight of the new cars ran in the Paris–Vienna race, Henri Farman finishing second overall and winning the *grande voiture* class. In speed over fairly level ground the Panhards were well ahead of their rivals, de Knyff averaging 54·4 m.p.h. for the first leg of the race from Paris to Belfort. The next big success for the Panhard came in the Circuit des Ardennes when Charles

11 **NAPIER,** 1902, Great Britain

Napier's first racing car was also their first four-cylinder machine, and ran unsuccessfully in the 1900 Paris–Toulouse–Paris race. For 1901 they built an enormous, unwieldy machine of 50 h.p. It weighed 1800 kg., making it by far the heaviest racing car of that season. It was no more successful than its predecessor, and for 1902 Napier produced a much lower, more compact car with shaft drive, rated at 30 h.p. This was chosen as Great Britain's repre-sentative in the Gordon Bennett Race which was run concurrently with part of the Paris–Vienna route, over the section to Innsbruck. S. F. Edge, the main sales agent and famous publicist for Napier cars, was at the wheel. His only serious rival for the Cup was the Chevalier Rene de Knyff driving a 70-h.p. Panhard (10), but he was a very formid-able rival, having led the whole field as far as Belfort. Later the Panhard's differential failed, and Edge had only to carry on to Innsbruck to win the Gordon Bennett Cup for Britain. The total cost of the exercise, including the purchase of the car, was estimated at

£1418, of which £1200 was recovered by the subsequent sale of the Napier. For the 1903 Gordon Bennett Race, held in Ireland, Napier fielded two 7·7-litre cars, based on the 1902 model, and a completely new 80-h.p., 13-litre car which Edge himself drove. None was successful. The 30-h.p. Gordon Bennett engine was used in a touring Napier introduced in the summer of 1903 and listed at a chassis price of £1200.

12 SERPOLLET, 1902, France

In the early days of record-breaking, the internal combustion engine took third place to steam and electricity. The original records for the flying kilometre were established by the electric cars of de Chasseloup-Laubat and Jenatzy (3, 2), and the next successful contender was Léon Serpollet in a special short-chassis steam car known as 'Easter Egg'. He had covered the flying kilometre in 35·8 seconds in 1901, and in 1902 he reduced this time to 29·8 seconds, equal to a speed of 75·6 m.p.h. This was 10 m.p.h. faster than Jenatzy's record set up three years before. Serpollet took over a kilometre to bring the car to a standstill after this record. In September 1902 Le Blon covered the flying kilometre uphill at Gaillon in 40·8 seconds, and a fortnight later in 36 seconds. These figures beat all those of internal combustion cars. Impressive though these speeds were, Serpollet could not claim that steam was really a rival to petrol until his cars held their own in long-distance events, and this he never succeeded in doing. Two

cars ran in Paris–Berlin in 1901 but retired early on, and the marque's next appearance was in the 1902 Circuit du Nord alcohol race, when four Serpollets were entered. They all completed the 537-mile course, but were behind the Panhards of Farman and Jarrott. Four cars again ran in Paris–Vienna and again all four finished, though the highest position was Chanliaud's fifteenth place. For 1903 Serpollet prepared larger cars whose engines were rated at 40 n.h.p. compared with 15 n.h.p. for the 1902 machines. Seven of these started in Paris–Madrid, and all finished, though not among the leaders. This in a sense reversed the impression given by Serpollets in earlier years, showing that they were reliable over long distances, but not fast enough to hold their own with the best internal-combustion engined cars. Three of the 40-h.p. cars (illustrated), ran in the Circuit des Ardennes of 1903, and Le Blon finished fourth. The last racing Serpollets were the six-cylinder machines built for the 1904 Gordon Bennett Eliminating Trials. Only one of these completed the course (Le Blon), and he was not fast enough to gain a place in the French team. An appearance at the Gaillon hill-climb in the autumn of 1904 marked the end of Serpollet's competition activity.

13 WINTON, 1903, U.S.A.

Like many other early manufacturers, Alexander Winton entered the motor business via the bicycle industry. He produced his first car in 1897, seven years after he set up his bicycle factory in Cleveland, Ohio. His first racing car was built for the 1900 Gordon Bennett Race and had an enormous horizontal single-cylinder engine of 3·8 litres' capacity. It failed to make any impression, but Winton was aware of the publicity value of racing, and for the 1903 Gordon Bennett he prepared two highly unusual cars. Known as the Winton Bullets, they had in-line engines lying on their sides, a four of $8\frac{1}{2}$ litres' capacity and and an eight with the same cylinder dimensions, giving 17 litres. They had pneumatic governors, and the larger car, driven by Winton himself, had only one forward speed. Their performance in the Gordon Bennett Race was undistinguished. Winton started 40 minutes late owing to a choked carburettor jet, and retired on the fourth lap, while Percy Owen on the 40-h.p. car struggled on for one further lap before retiring with overheating. His car was described as a 'veritable furnace'. Like the other American Gordon Bennett entry, the Peerless, the Winton Bullets had a better career in their home country. Barney Oldfield in the eight-cylinder car set a new record for the mile in 55 seconds and for 10 miles in 9 minutes 45 seconds.

14 GOBRON-BRILLIÉ, 1903, France

The most unusual characteristic of Gobron-Brillié cars was their engine of opposed-piston design. Each cylinder contained two pistons, the explosion taking place between them and driving the lower piston downwards in the usual way and the upper piston upwards. The lower was attached to a conventional crankshaft, while the upper

was linked to it by crossheads and connecting-rods. This system was claimed to eliminate vibration, and was found on all Gobron cars up to 1922. The firm supported racing from 1900 onwards, entering two-cylinder cars in Paris–Toulouse–Paris, Paris–Berlin, and Paris–Vienna, as well as the Circuit du Nord alcohol race of 1902. The latter fuel was particularly suited to the Gobron-Brillié, and their 1901 catalogue claimed that the cars would perform well on gin, brandy, or whisky. In 1903 came a much larger car, the four-cylinder, eight-piston machine illustrated, with a capacity of $13\frac{1}{2}$-litres and a lightweight tubular frame. This model had an undistinguished racing career but was unbeatable in short distance events such as sprints and hill-climbs. Its leading drivers were Louis Rigolly and Arthur Duray. Between them they broke the World's Land Speed Record four times, Duray reaching 83·47 m.p.h. at Ostend in July 1903 and 84·73 m.p.h. at Dourdan in November. In 1904 Rigolly recorded 94·78 m.p.h. at Nice in March, and at Ostend in July became the first man officially to exceed 100 m.p.h. in a motor-car, with a speed of 103·55 m.p.h. He continued to drive his Gobron-Brillié in races, running in the 1904 and 1905 Gordon Bennett Eliminating Trials and, incredibly, in the 1906 and 1907 Grands Prix. He would have entered the old car in the 1908 Grand Prix as well, but the limitation on piston area in that year's formula was naturally awkward for a double piston engine and the Gobron was ineligible. The company built no new cars for the Grands Prix, and the name was not seen again in racing. Strictly speaking the cars were no longer Gobron-Brilliés after 1903 when Eugène Brillié left the firm, but were generally so called up to the First World War. After the war, they were invariably called Gobrons. Production ceased in 1929.

represent France. This honour went to the sister Turcat-Méry of Rougier, also of 12·8 litres but officially listed as a 100-h.p. car. After 1906, De Dietrich cars were known as Lorraine-Dietrich (60).

15 DE DIETRICH, 1903, France

The De Dietrich company had factories at Niederbronn in German Alsace and at Lunéville in French Lorraine. The German factory built the Amédée Bollée (1) under licence and later made Bugatti-designed cars from 1903 to 1905, while the French firm also used outside designs, from the Marseilles manufacturers Turcat *et* Méry. They were conventional cars on Panhard lines with front-mounted vertical engines, tubular radiators, flitch-plate frames, and chain drive. Three 16-h.p., 4·1-litre *voitures légères* ran in Paris–Vienna in 1902 and for the 1903 Paris–Madrid race the firm entered three 5·8-litre, 30-h.p. and seven 9·9-litre, 45-h.p. cars. These had mixed fortunes: Charles Jarrott finished third on a 45 h.p., four failed to finish and on one of them Loraine Barrow was killed. The 30-h.p. cars did better, all three finishing; Mouter in twelfth place, Lafont seventieth and Mme du Gast, the only lady driver in the race, seventy-seventh. In addition to these, Rougier drove a 45-h.p. Turcat-Méry, which was the same design, into eleventh place. In the Circuit des Ardennes, de Brou was third on a 45-h.p. De Dietrich. The cars entered in the 1904 Gordon Bennett Eliminating Trials were of 80 h.p. and 12·8 litres, but they were not chosen to

16 DE DION BOUTON, 1903, France

De Dion tricycles dominated the motor-cycle classes of the early town-to-town races and frequently did well against four-wheeled cars, but from 1900 onwards the firm took relatively little part in racing, although commercially they were France's most important manufacturers. The prototype of the front-engined single-cylinder car ran in the touring class of the 1901 Paris–Berlin race, although the model was not put on the market until 1902. For the 1903 Paris–Madrid race De Dion entered four *voitures légères* with 18-h.p., four-cylinder engines of 3 litres' capacity. They were the first fours made by the company, and it was not until 1905 that a four-cylinder touring De Dion was offered for sale to the public. In addition to the *voitures légères* (illustrated), there were three De Dions in the *voiturette* class, with 9-h.p. single-cylinder engines of 1021-cc. capacity. Both models had tubular frames, the familiar De Dion rear axles and shaft drive. Pélisson's 18 h.p. finished fifth in his class, while Holley's 9 h.p. was fifth in the *voiturette* category. Three 18-h.p. cars ran in the 1903 Circuit des Ardennes, finishing sixth, seventh, and tenth, but the firm gave racing a miss in 1904, returning in 1905 to support the first Coupe de *l'Auto* for light cars.

This had a capacity limit of 1 litre, so the only eligible De Dion was the 100 × 120-mm. single of 940 cc. This led to a series of single-cylinder racing cars up to 1908 (43), but the fours raced no more.

17 MERCEDES, 1903,
Germany

The first car to bear the name Mercedes appeared in 1901 as a result of Emil Jellinek's dissatisfaction with the unstable Cannstatt-Daimler Phoenix racing cars (4). Named after Jellinek's eldest daughter, the Mercedes had a 5·9-litre, 35-h.p. pair-cast four-cylinder engine, honeycomb radiator, mechanically operated inlet valves, selective gear change, and pressed steel frame. It was an advanced but not freakish design, and set the pattern for expensive cars for years to come. Among those who found inspiration in the Mercedes for both their touring and racing models were F.I.A.T. in Italy, Rochet-Schneider in France, Star in England, and Locomobile in the United States. The first sporting appearance of the new car was in the Grand Prix de Pau in February 1901. It was an ignominious beginning to a glorious career, for the car was ill-prepared and retired a few yards from the start with a faulty clutch. One of the old Phoenix Daimlers was also entered as a Mercedes, and this crashed during the race. A few weeks later, during the Nice Speed Week, Wilhelm Werner in a Mercedes 35 h.p. defeated all the gasoline-engined cars over the flying kilometre and also won the Nice–Salon–Nice race. Hill-climb successes at La Turbie and Semmering

followed, and more laurels were earned by the 1902 Mercedes, whose engine was boosted to 40 h.p. and 6·8 litres. Count Eliot Zborowski was second in Paris–Vienna, although defeated by Marcel Renault's light car (8). In 1903 came the 60-h.p. machine illustrated, with inlet-over-exhaust engine of 9·2 litres and top speed of 75 m.p.h. An early model of this reduced the record for the La Turbie hill-climb by $3\frac{1}{2}$ minutes, and another won the standing start mile at Nice, but for the Paris–Madrid race six even larger cars of 90 h.p. and nearly 12 litres' capacity were entered, as well as six 60s. They proved disappointing (Mercedes' best performance in the race was Warden's fifth place on a 60) and it was perhaps fortunate that the 90-h.p. Gordon Bennett cars were destroyed in a fire at the factory. Three stripped touring 60s were entered, and Jenatzy's won at 49·2 m.p.h. from de Knyff's Panhard. The Baron de Caters, in another 60, was fifth. In the Irish Fortnight that followed the Gordon Bennett races, 60-h.p. Mercedes took two fastest times of the day in sprints.

In 1904 the 90 was the Cannstatt company's front-line car, but the 60 continued to do well in private hands. Vincenzo Florio was third in the Coppa Florio, and Algernon Lee Guinness made fastest time of the day at the Brighton Speed Trials. The model did well in touring car events also, for those were the days when the same chassis might carry racing, touring, and limousine bodywork. Willy Poege was third in the 1905 Herkomer Trial for touring cars. Several Mercedes 60s survive, including the Nice Speed Week car now fitted with a tourer body and loaned to the Montagu Motor Museum, by whom it is regularly entered in the London to Brighton veteran car run.

18 NAPIER, 1904, Great Britain

Although the first six-cylinder touring Napier appeared in 1903, it was not until the summer of the following year that a six-cylinder racing car appeared. This had a 15·1-litre, 90-h.p. engine and two-speed gear-box, and was used by S. F. Edge in practice for the 1904 Gordon Bennett Race, although in the event itself he drove one of the old 80-h.p., four-cylinder cars. The six, known as L48, originally had a typical Napier radiator, but this was soon replaced by a tubular radiator which was wrapped around the bonnet to give a striking appearance. Later in 1904 Arthur Macdonald made fastest time of the day at Portmarnock Speed Trials, and in 1905 he established six world records at the Ormond-Daytona Beach meeting in Florida. These included the flying mile at 104·65 m.p.h. The Napier was the fastest British car at the time, and was chosen for the 1905 Gordon Bennett Race, to be driven by Clifford Earp. However, its two-speed gear-box was a handicap on the mountainous Auvergne circuit, and it finished no higher than ninth. Earp took the car to America again in 1906, but had less success than Macdonald the previous year, the opposition including the 200-h.p. Darracq vee-eight (21) and the Stanley steamer (22). In 1907 the Napier's stroke was increased from 127 mm. to 178 mm., giving a capacity of over 20-litres. Now known as

Samson, it was driven by Frank Newton at Brooklands, where it broke the 90-h.p. short record at 119·34 m.p.h. It was matched against Felice Nazzaro's 89·5-h.p. Fiat *Mephistopheles*, but retired with a broken crankshaft.

19 RICHARD-BRASIER, 1904, 1905, France

Richard-Brasier cars were made by Georges Richard and designed by Henri Brasier who had formerly been with Mors (7). Strictly speaking, they were only made in 1903 and 1904, as in the latter year Georges Richard left the firm to make cars under the name Unic, but the name Richard-Brasier stuck, certainly for the two Gordon Bennett cars illustrated. Brasier's first racing design for Georges Richard was a 12-h.p., four-cylinder, shaft-driven *voiturette*. Four ran in Paris–Madrid; Barillier was second in his class. A 6·8-litre car followed later in 1903, on which Danjean won his class in the Dourdan Speed Trials, and in 1904 there appeared the 80-h.p. car shown in the top illustration. It had a 9·9-litre 'T'-head engine, pressed steel frame, and chain drive. Léon Théry won the French Eliminating Trials for the Gordon Bennett, in which twenty-nine cars from ten factories took part, and he went on to win the race itself. It was remarked that the Richard-Brasier was very smooth and held the road remarkably well, thanks to the use of shock absorbers. It has been said that the smooth running of the 1904 Richard-Brasier led Mercedes to consider employing shock absorbers on their own racing cars, although they did not do so until 1907. For the 1905 Gordon

Bennett, Brasier built a lower car with a larger engine of 96 h.p. Three of these ran in the Eliminating Trials and two were selected for the race, driven by Théry and Caillois. Again Théry was the winner, while his team-mate was fourth. Brasiers ran in the first three Grands Prix, their best result being Baras' third in 1907.

20 WOLSELEY, 1905, Great Britain

Herbert Austin's horizontal-engined Wolseleys were among the most distinctive British cars of the 1900 to 1905 period. Moreover, in 1902 Wolseley was the country's largest motor manufacturer. Austin was one of the very select band of British designers whose racing cars were regularly seen in European events. A large chain-driven racing car with four-cylinder engine and five-speed gear-box was built in 1901 but not raced. However, in 1902, two racing models appeared, a 6·4-litre, 30-h.p., four-cylinder and an 8·2-litre, 45-h.p. with only three cylinders, surely the largest three-cylinder car ever made. Both were entered for Paris–Vienna, but only the 30-h.p. car started, driven by Austin himself. He twice suffered the misfortune of a broken crankshaft, and it is not surprising that after the second breakage he retired. The four-cylinder engine was enlarged to 11·1 litres in 1903, and three of these cars started in Paris–Madrid. Herbert Austin and Harvey Foster retired, while Leslie Porter had a bad accident in which his mechanic was killed. The car did no better in the Circuit des Ardennes, and for 1904 two new designs were pre-

pared. One had a horizontally-opposed engine as in the 1903 cars, but with capacity enlarged to 11·9 litres, while the other had the same capacity but an in-line engine mounted transversely. The former was known as the 72 h.p., the latter as the 96 h.p. The extra power was probably due to the use of lighter reciprocating parts in the 96 h.p. and a higher engine speed (1500 r.p.m. compared with 1000 r.p.m.), although some sources say that the 96 h.p. had a longer stroke of $6\frac{1}{2}$ in. against the 6 in. of the 72 h.p. None of these cars survives, so it is impossible to check today. Sidney Girling's 72 h.p. and Charles Jarrott's 96 h.p. were selected to run in the Gordon Bennett Race. Girling finished ninth and Jarrott, whose car had a longer bonnet, giving it the nickname *Beetle*, finished twelfth. Two 96-h.p. cars ran in the 1905 Gordon Bennett, driven by C. S. Rolls and Cecil Bianchi, the former finishing eighth. This was the highest-placed British car. 1905 was the last year in which the Wolseleys were raced, as the company felt that the rewards of racing, even if successful, were not worth the enormous expense of maintaining a full racing department. Anyway, Austin left the following year to make cars under his own name, and the later Wolseley-Siddeleys had vertical engines.

21 DARRACQ, 1905, France

Alexandre Darracq supported racing keenly from 1901 onwards, building such diverse machinery as the 12-h.p. *voiturette* which won its class in Paris–Vienna in 1902, and the 100-h.p., 11·2-

litre Gordon Bennett Trials car of 1904. The latter was not successful on a circuit, but did much better in sprints, Baras covering a flying kilometre at 104·52 m.p.h. The lure of the monster sprint car led Alexandre Darracq to build an eight-cylinder car in 1905, using two blocks of the Gordon Bennett engine in vee formation. This engine had a capacity of 22,518 cc. and developed 200 b.h.p. at 1200 r.p.m. The sixteen valves were all overhead. This engine was mounted in a very light chassis of 7 ft. 10 in. wheelbase and a wide track of 5 ft. 1 in. Victor Hémery set a record of 109·65 m.p.h. for the flying kilometre on the Arles–Salon road. Algernon Lee Guinness later bought the car and raised this record to 117·66 m.p.h. at Ostend in July 1906.

22 STANLEY, 1906, U.S.A.

The Stanley was the best-known and longest-lived American steam car, and for several years the Stanley twins who built it were actively interested in racing and record-breaking. They entered competitions in 1902 with the little 5½-h.p. folding-front seat tourers, which often defeated larger and more expensive gasoline-engined cars, and the following year there appeared the first of the streamlined cars known variously as *Wogglebug*, *Teakettle*, *Rocket*, and *Beetle*. The *Wogglebug* covered the mile in 1 minute 2·8 seconds at Readville Track, Boston, and this performance was followed by Louis S. Ross' mile in 38 seconds (94·73 m.p.h.) at Daytona in January 1905 with *Teakettle*. These streamlined Stanleys looked more like upturned boats than motor-cars,

but their engines were not dissimilar to those used in production touring cars. The most famous of them all, Fred Marriott's *Rocket* (illustrated), used a 20-h.p., two-cylinder engine mounted behind, and geared directly to, the rear axle. The driving gear wheel had 82 teeth and meshed with one of 48 teeth. This engine weighed only 200 lb. With this car Marriott covered the mile in 28·2 seconds, equal to a speed of 127·66 m.p.h., nearly 20 m.p.h. faster than the existing World's Land Speed Record set up by Hémery in the 200-h.p. Darracq (21). However, because the run was not carried out under A.I.A.C.R. rules, it was not recognized officially. The following year Marriott was back at Daytona with a slightly modified *Rocket*. In attempting to beat his own record his car hit a depression in the sand, crashed, and was totally destroyed, although Marriott escaped with his life. His speed just before the crash has been claimed to be as high as 190 m.p.h., but is more likely to have been in the region of 150 m.p.h. After this accident the Stanleys abandoned record-breaking. They built a much more conventional looking racing car for the Vanderbilt Cup, but it never reached the starting line, and after 1906 they no longer went in for sport, although privately-owned roadsters had many successes in hillclimbs for a number of years.

23 CLÉMENT-BAYARD, 1906, France

Adolphe Clément was a noted company promoter in the world of bicycles and pneumatic tires before he turned to motor-cars, and was one of the first men to make a fortune from the new means of transport. In 1904 he began a serious racing programme, entering two four-cylinder cars of 80 h.p. (11·3 litres) and one of 100 h.p. (16·3 litres) in the Gordon Bennett Eliminating Trials. The smaller had shaft drive, but the larger drove by chains. One of the 80-h.p. cars was driven by Clément's nineteen-year-old son Albert, who was the leading driver for the marque until his death during practice for the 1907 Grand Prix. Neither Clément-Bayard was chosen to represent France in the Gordon Bennett, but the smaller was seen again in the Circuit des Ardennes, in which event Clément also fielded two 30-h.p. *voitures légères* and an 18-h.p. *voiturette* which won its class. An 80 h.p. also ran in the Vanderbilt Cup, in which Albert Clément finished second. For the 1905 Eliminating Trials Clément produced two new shaft-driven racing cars with square cylinder dimensions which developed 100 h.p. from 12·9 litres. They were no more successful than the 1904 cars in the Trials, but Clément's faith in them was justified in the first of the Grands Prix the following year. Albert Clément lay second at the end of the first day's racing, and finished third overall. Later in the year he was sixth in the Circuit des Ardennes and fourth in the Vanderbilt Cup. Three of the same cars ran in the 1907 Grand Prix, but Albert was killed in practice, and the best they could manage was Garcet's eighth place. For 1908 a new Grand Prix car was built, with a single overhead camshaft and hemispherical combustion chambers. They were among the fastest cars on the Dieppe circuit but had severe tire troubles, and their best position was fourth.

24 **HOTCHKISS,** 1906, France

The Hotchkiss company was never renowned for racing cars, and the marque did not really make a name for itself in motor sport until its string of Monte Carlo Rally successes in the 1930s and 1940s. But despite the directors' dictum that 'racing is the curse of the automobile trade', the company did build some large competition cars in its early days, notably for the 1904 Gordon Bennett Race and the 1906 Grand Prix. The 1904 cars had 17,813 cc., four-cylinder engines, chain drive, and pointed Mors-like bonnets with the radiators beneath. They were not successful in the Eliminating Trials, but Le Blon drove one into fifth place in the Circuit des Ardennes, and they did well in sprints and hill-climbs. The 1905 Hotchkisses had even larger engines of 18·8 litres, shaft drive, and the familiar round radiator which characterized the marque for many years. Like their predecessors, they were not chosen to represent France in the Gordon Bennett Race. For the 1906 Grand Prix the company prepared three cars with 16·3-litre engines and wire wheels, being one of only two makes in the race to use the latter feature (the other was Darracq). The drivers were Le Blon, Salleron, and the American Elliot Shepard, who was fourth at the end of the first day but retired later. Neither of his team-mates completed the first day's racing. Shepard subsequently took his car to America and entered it in the Vanderbilt Cup, in which he crashed. However, it was rebuilt and had a long career in the hands of George Robertson and others. One of the other Grand Prix Hotchkisses was seen at Brooklands in 1909.

The company did not enter a car in the 1907 Grand Prix, and in fact never made a racing car again.

25 LOCOMOBILE, 1906, U.S.A.

The first products of the Locomobile Company of America were light steam cars built to Stanley designs, but a gasoline car designed by A. L. Riker was introduced in 1902, and by 1905 Locomobile followed the Mercedes layout of a four-cylinder 'T'-head engine, honeycomb radiator, and double-chain drive. They entered European racing with a 17,657-cc. car which Joe Tracy drove in the 1905 Gordon Bennett Race. Unfortunately, second gear had been broken during the drive to the race, and in the mountainous Auvergne country this was a fatal handicap. Tracy retired on the third lap. However, in the Vanderbilt Cup in October 1905 he finished third. This encouraged Riker and the Locomobile company to build another car for the 1906 Cup. Slightly smaller at 16 litres' capacity, it had an inlet-over-exhaust valve engine and developed at least as much power as the 1905 car. It easily won the Eliminating Trials from seven other American makes, and with Thomas (40), Frayer-Miller, Christie (28), and Haynes, was chosen to represent America in the Vanderbilt Cup. Tracy again drove, but although his was the fastest car in the race he was delayed by eleven tire changes and finished only tenth. Strictly speaking, he did not finish at all, as he was in tenth place when the race was stopped because of the crowd flocking on to the course. There was no

Vanderbilt Cup in 1907, but for the 1908 race the two-year-old car was entered again, this time with George Robertson, a twenty-three-year-old New Yorker, at the wheel. Despite tire trouble which dropped him to fourth at one point in the race, Robertson won at an average speed of 64·2 m.p.h. This was the first time that an American car had won a major race against the best European opposition. The car bore the number 16 in the race, and ever since then it has been known as 'Old 16'. It was bought from the company by Joseph Sessions, head of a foundry which had made Locomobile castings, and owned by him until 1941 when it passed into the hands of Peter Helck, the distinguished motor racing artist.

26 RENAULT, 1906, France

After the death of Marcel Renault at the wheel of a 30-h.p. car in the 1903 Paris–Madrid race (8), Louis abandoned racing for two years. The only racing car to come from the Billancourt works in 1904 was a 60-h.p. machine with circular dashboard radiator built to the special order of the American millionaire Gould Brokaw. By 1905 Louis could no longer resist the lure of racing, and entered three cars for the Gordon Bennett Eliminating Trials. These had 90-h.p. four-cylinder engines of 12,975 cc., with underslung frames and pump cooling. The chassis consisted of deep section steel frames, curved to the body shape, above which were riveted the upper parts of the body. This was an early form of monocoque construction. Unfortunately, the pump cooling was inadequate and all three cars overheated badly, so that they were not chosen for the Gordon Bennett Race. For the first of the Grands Prix in 1906 Renault built the new design illustrated. This retained the 90-h.p. engine but abandoned the troublesome pump cooling in favour of thermo-syphon, and also replaced the underslung 'semi-monocoque' frame with a conventional separate chassis. Michelin quick detachable rims were used at the rear, and in practice the Renaults used wire wheels, but replaced these with artillery type for the race itself. Three cars were entered in the Grand Prix, driven by the Hungarian Ferenc Szisz, Edmond, and Richez. The latter pair retired, but Szisz won at 62·92 m.p.h. This earned him and the firm of Renault undying fame as the victors in the first Grand Prix of all, though curiously neither man nor car became leading lights in the later history of Grand Prix racing. Renault used the same design for the 1907 Grand Prix, though now with detachable rims all round. Szisz finished second to Felice Nazzaro's Fiat (29). The basic design lasted a further year, although the engine had to be modified slightly to accommodate the new bore limitations of 155 mm. A longer stroke combined with the reduced bore to give a slightly smaller capacity of 12,076 cc., but power was up to 105 h.p. at the higher engine speed of 2000 r.p.m. However, Szisz's car was hampered by tire changing problems and the best the marque could do was the eighth place of the newcomer Dmitri. The cars ran again in the American Grand Prize at Savannah, Georgia, and Herbert Strang finished sixth. This was their last competition appearance, and Renault never built a Grand Prix car again. As for

Szisz, he drove for a few more years in Alda and Lorraine-Dietrich cars, and then enjoyed an exceptionally long retirement, dying in 1970 at the age of ninety-seven.

27 DARRACQ, 1906, France

The ancestry of the 1906 Grand Prix Darracqs can be traced back to the 11·2-litre cars built for the 1904 Gordon Bennett Eliminating Trials. These were raced as Darracqs in France, and similar designs built in Germany and Scotland raced under the names Opel-Darracq and Weir-Darracq respectively. This was Alexandre Darracq's attempt to see that at least one of his cars ran in the Gordon Bennett, but in fact the Darracqs and Weir-Darracqs performed dismally in their countries' Eliminating Trials. Even the Opel-Darracq retired on the first lap. The 1905 Darracqs used slightly smaller engines of 9896 cc. rated at 80 h.p. They had overhead valves operated by exposed push-rods and rockers, and very light chassis which were said to have been derived from the firm's small touring cars. The wheelbase was 7 ft. 10 in. and the track a wide 5 ft. 1 in. which gave the cars a curiously square appearance. There was no differential, and the three-speed gearchange was mounted in the rear axle. Three cars ran in the Eliminating Trial, and Wagner's was the fastest; alas, he was delayed by tire troubles and finished only fourth, so no Darracqs ran in the race itself. The same engine, enlarged again to 12,711 cc. was used in the 1906 Grand Prix car illustrated. Its appearance was very different, however, for it had a large vee-radiator similar to that of the 200-h.p., vee-eight car (21), and also had the latter's upswept frame at the rear. Three of these cars ran in the Grand Prix, driven by Hanriot, Hémery, and Wagner, but only Hémery survived the first day's racing, and even he did not complete the second day. This disappointing performance was somewhat redeemed by Hémery's second place in the Circuit des Ardennes.

28 CHRISTIE, 1907, U.S.A.

The racing cars of John Walter Christie were among the most unusual to grace any track on either side of the Atlantic. Christie was a keen adherent of the front-wheel-drive principle, and also of the transverse mounting of engines. On his racing cars the wheels were driven directly from the ends of the crankshaft, which took the place of a front axle. Cornering was facilitated by slipping the inside wheel clutch, as there was no differential. There was no conventional radiator, but the Christie had an enormous radiator blanket wrapped around the bonnet behind the engine. The first Christie racing cars of 1904-5 had in-line four-cylinder engines, and these were followed by the Double Ender, with two 60-h.p., four-cylinder engines, one in front driving the front wheels, and one behind the driver which powered the rear wheels. With the rear engine removed Christie drove this car in the 1905 Vanderbilt Cup, in which he retired after a crash. For 1906 he employed a vee-four engine of 13 litres' capacity, and in 1907 enlarged this to nearly 20 litres. This was the car (illustrated) which he brought

to Europe for the 1907 Grand Prix. He came with an awesome reputation, including a claimed maximum speed of 120 m.p.h., but his shatteringly noisy car was never among the leaders, its roadholding was poor, and on the fifth lap Christie retired with a sticking exhaust valve. He had no team-mates, and in fact drove himself on every occasion when his cars appeared up to 1907. After the Grand Prix Christie gave up entering major events, and took his cars on tour of the United States, giving demonstrations on dirt tracks at local fairs. One of his drivers in this period, which lasted up to 1910, was the famous Barney Oldfield. Christie never made passenger cars in series, but achieved considerable fame making two-wheeled powered attachments for fire engines, and in the 1930s he designed some high-speed tanks. He died in 1944.

29 FIAT, 1907, Italy

The famous Turin firm, Fabbrica Italiana Automobili Torino, was among a number of European and American manufacturers who followed the successful Mercedes pattern (17), and their racing cars of the 1904-8 period bore an unmistakable resemblance to the cars from Cannstatt. For the 1904 Gordon Bennett Race F.I.A.T. (the periods were dropped from the name after 1906) sent three 10,568-cc., four-cylinder chain-driven cars with inlet-over-exhaust valve engines; their best result was Vincenzo Lancia's eighth place. The 1905 F.I.A.T.s were logical developments of the 1904 cars, but with larger engines of 16·3 litres' capacity and all-overhead valves. They performed much better in the Gordon Bennett, Lancia leading the race until his retirement on the third lap, and his team-mates Nazzaro and Cagno finishing second and third. Similar cars ran in the 1906 Grand Prix, Nazzaro finishing second and Lancia fifth. For 1907 the stroke was shortened by 10 mm. to 150 mm. giving a capacity of 15,268 cc. Three cars (illustrated) were entered in the Grand Prix, driven by Nazzaro, Lancia, and Wagner. Wagner led the race for three laps before retiring, and Lancia had a neck-and-neck duel with Duray's de Dietrich at the head of the field for two laps. Eventually Duray fell out with gear-box trouble, Lancia had a slipping clutch, and it was Nazzaro's Fiat that won. This victory was backed up by Nazzaro's triumph in the Targa Florio and the Kaiserpreis in smaller Fiats. Altogether it was an excellent season for Fiat, and established them as one of the leading sporting marques as well as respected makers of luxury touring cars.

30 DUFAUX, 1907, Switzerland

The 1907 Grand Prix was notable for unorthodox machinery; in addition to Christie's vee-four (28) there were three cars with straight-eight engines: the English Weigel, the French Porthos, and the Swiss Dufaux. The latter was, in fact, the last of a series of straight-eight racing cars which the brothers Frédéric and Charles Dufaux of Geneva had been building since 1904. Their first car was made in the Piccard-Pictet (74) works, and had a $12\frac{3}{4}$-litre engine with pair-cast cylinders. It was entered for the Gordon Bennett Race but did not

start, and the same disappointment attended their 1905 Gordon Bennett entry. However, Frédéric Dufaux had a number of successes in sprints. Apart from an extraordinary 26·4-litre, four-cylinder car of 1905 which never raced, Dufaux built no more competition cars until 1907, when they entered a straight-eight for the Grand Prix. This (illustrated) was called a 120-h.p. car, but was in fact identical to the 1904 car, which was rated at 70/90 h.p. Driven by Frédéric Dufaux, it was never among the leaders, but lasted for seven of the ten laps. Dufaux made no more racing cars after 1907, and indeed production of their touring cars ceased at about the same time.

31 PIPE, 1907, Belgium

The Pipe from Ghent was not as well-known a Belgian car as the Minerva (34) or Excelsior (63), but it was a high-quality machine, and the firm's racing cars had some advanced features. They were first seen in 1901 in the Paris–Berlin race, but the more significant Pipes appeared in 1903, running in Paris–Madrid and the Circuit des Ardennes. These had 7·2-litre, four-cylinder engines with mechanically-operated overhead valves and magnetic clutches of Jenatzy design. They failed to finish in Paris–Madrid but were seventh and eighth in the Ardennes. The 1904 Gordon Bennett cars were even more interesting, with inclined overhead valves and hemispherical combustion chambers like the 1912 Peugeots (65). Unlike the Peugeots they did not have overhead camshafts, but it was nevertheless a most advanced design for 1904. Capacity of the four-cylinder engines was $13\frac{1}{2}$-litres and output 60 b.h.p. With one of these cars, Hautvast was sixth in the Gordon Bennett Race. A similar valve arrangement and head design was used in the 8-litre cars entered in the 1907 Kaiserpreis (illustrated), and in this event Hautvast finished in second place, being beaten only by Nazzaro's Fiat. His team-mate Deplus managed to get into the final but retired on the fourth lap. Three cars ran in the 1907 Circuit des Ardennes, when drivers included the great Jenatzy, but all retired. Pipe never contested the Grands Prix, and after 1907 they were seen only in touring events.

32 BERLIET, 1907, France

The famous Lyon firm of Berliet never took a great deal of interest in racing, and were almost unique among their contemporaries in not supporting any of the town-to-town races of 1895 to 1903, nor in entering any of the Grands Prix. However, they entered local hill-climbs from 1904 onwards, and in 1906 Paul Bablot drove a 40-h.p. Berliet into third place in the Targa Florio. He was also second in a 22-h.p. tourer in the Royal Automobile Club's Tourist Trophy race in the Isle of Man. Berliet seemed more interested in Italian races than any others, for they fielded two cars in 1907 Targa Florio, neither of which lasted the first lap, and one in 1908, driven by Porporato, finished in fourth place. Later in 1908 Porporato gained Berliet's greatest triumph in racing with a victory in the 262-mile

Targa Bologna. A number of the large 40-h.p. Berliets were sold to private owners who used them in hill-climbs, and the car illustrated is one of these. Said to be a reserve car built for the 1907 Kaiserpreis race, it was imported into Australia in the same year, and had a two-speed rear axle.

33 MARTINI, 1907, Switzerland

Probably the best-known product of the Martini company was their rifle, but they also made textile machinery, stationary engines, and motor-cars. The latter first appeared in 1897, and by 1903 a hundred cars a year were being turned out. The company's first sporting feat was the ascent of the rack railway from Montreux to Rochers de Naye, with gradients of up to 1 in 4. This was achieved by a 16-h.p., four-cylinder tourer made under licence from the French Rochet-Schneider company whose cars were, in turn, fairly close copies of the Mercedes. The next sporting effort of Martini was the entry of two cars in the 1907 Kaiserpreis race. Although the race was for cars nominally of touring type, the Martinis (illustrated) were specially prepared. They had $7\frac{1}{2}$-litre, four-cylinder engines rated at 80 h.p. and chain drive. One was driven by Beutler, who was a director of the Martini company, and the other by Beck, who also drove the little overhead-camshaft Martini *voiturette* in 1908 (39). Both Martinis reached the final of the Kaiserpreis, and finished twelfth (Beutler) and fifteenth (Beck). The cars were in fact only 13 seconds apart at the finish. As only two Swiss cars were entered, they could claim 100 per cent finishing success, a better record than that of any other country.

34 MINERVA, 1907, Belgium

The Minerva was one of the finest cars made in Belgium, and was one of a number of European makes firmly established in the public mind as a supporter of the sleeve-valve principle. However, this was only introduced in 1909, and like Daimler in England, Minerva had a more sporting image in their pre-sleeve valve days. They prepared a team of three 8-litre, four-cylinder cars with inlet-over-exhaust valve engines and chain drive for the 1907 Kaiserpreis, but none reached the final. However, a team of four similar cars ran in the Circuit des Ardennes a month later and scored a striking success, with first, second, third, and sixth places. The drivers were, respectively, J. T. C. Moore-Brabazon (later Lord Brabazon of Tara), Koolhoven, Algernon Lee Guinness, and Warwick Wright. Although the same cars, driven by Porlier and Moore-Brabazon, came first and second in the less important Liederkerke Cup, the Circuit des Ardennes remained Minerva's greatest sporting triumph. After the introduction of sleeve valves in 1909 they confined their sporting activities largely to rallies, where they had some success in the Swedish Winter Trials and Austrian Alpine Trials of 1911 to 1914. They did, however, run three 3·3-litre sleeve-valve racing cars in the 1914 Tourist Trophy, finishing second, third, and fifth.

35 NAPIER, 1908, Great Britain

Although Napier cars had been prominent in the Gordon Bennett Races (11, 18), S. F. Edge did not enter them for either of the first two Grands Prix. For 1908, however, he built three cars with $11\frac{1}{2}$-litre, six-cylinder engines. He fitted Rudge-Whitworth detachable wire wheels, which led to a storm resulting in the team's withdrawal from the race. The Automobile Club de France regarded the wheels as integral parts of the car which must not be changed, and only in 1906 had they permitted detachable rims (26). Edge accused the ACF of permitting detachable rims simply to aid the French cars, but this was ridiculous, as any manufacturer could have used them, although in fact only two did, Renault and Clément-Bayard. This accusation of bias infuriated the ACF, who flatly refused to countenance the Rudge-Whitworth wheels. Edge refused to modify the cars, and the entry was withdrawn. This was the nearest that Napier ever got to a Grand Prix appearance, for when the race was revived in 1912 the Acton firm was out of the competition world altogether. One of the Grand Prix cars was rebodied as a tourer and sold to America. A small number of replicas of the Grand Prix car were made, and one of these (illustrated) survives today.

36 ITALA, 1908, Italy

With the Fiat and Isotta Fraschini, the Itala was one of the finest Italian cars of the pre-1914 period. Although the original Itala of 1904 was in many ways similar to the Fiat, with four-cylinder 'T'-head engine and Mercedes-like radiator, it was unusual in using shaft drive on even the biggest models from the start. In 1905 an inlet-over-exhaust valve engine was used on the $15\frac{1}{2}$-litre Coppa Florio car with which Raggio won at 65·1 m.p.h. A smaller 40-h.p. car won the first Targa Florio in 1906. The driver was Alessandro Cagno, chauffeur to the Queen of Italy, who was Itala's most successful driver. The firm's most active period in racing was 1906 to 1908, when they supported the Grands Prix, Kaiserpreis, Coppa Florio, Targa Florio, Coppa della Velocita, and Vanderbilt Cup. They had mixed fortunes, winning the 1907 Coppa Velocita with Cagno at the wheel, but never finishing higher than eleventh in a Grand Prix (Cagno in 1908). The 1906 Grand Prix car was similar to the 1905 Coppa Florio model, and all three entries retired or crashed. Itala did not enter the 1907 Grand Prix, but built a big 14·4-litre car derived from the 1906 Grand Prix model for the Coppa della Velocita, which Cagno won at 65·2 m.p.h. This car survives today and can be seen at the Montagu Motor Museum at Beaulieu, Hants. For the 1908 Grand Prix Itala entered three cars (illustrated) similar to the Coppa Velocita model, but with slightly smaller engines at just over 12 litres' capacity. The drivers were Cagno, Henri Fournier, and Giovanni Piacenza, of whom Cagno was the only finisher.

37 MERCEDES, 1908, Germany

As one would expect from a name so closely connected with racing from its inception, Mercedes supported the first three Grands Prix with works teams of three cars each year. They all had four-cylinder inlet-over-exhaust valve engines, and the 1906 and 1907 cars were basically similar, both being derived from the 14-litre 1905 Gordon Bennett cars. They were not outstandingly successful in either Grand Prix, the best result being Hémery's tenth place in 1907. For 1908 Mercedes produced new cars with 12·8-litre, inlet-over-exhaust valve engines and high-tension ignition in place of the low-tension system used in their previous Grand Prix cars. One car had a 180-mm. stroke, giving $13\frac{1}{2}$-litres compared with 170 mm. for the other two. The three cars (illustrated) were driven by Willy Poege ($13\frac{1}{2}$ litre car), Christian Lautenschlager, and Otto Salzer. Lautenschlager took the lead on the fifth lap and never lost it, winning at 69·2 m.p.h. from two Benz cars driven by Hémery and Hanriot. Poege was fifth and Salzer, who had led for the first lap, retired on the second with a damaged rim. Two Grand Prix cars ran in the Vanderbilt Cup but did not do particularly well, and the best Mercedes performance in that event was Luttgen's fourth in an old '90'. There was no Grand Prix racing in 1909, but one of the Grand Prix cars had a considerable run of success in America in the hands of Ralph DePalma. He was second in the 1911 Vanderbilt Cup and third in the American Grand Prize, and in 1912 he won both the Vanderbilt Cup and the Elgin Trophy, and was third in the Indianapolis 500-Miles Race. The last appearance of the 1908 cars in European racing was in the 1913 Grand Prix de France at Le Mans, not to be confused with the

French Grand Prix which was run that year at Amiens. Their best result was the third place of Théodore Pilette, the Belgian agent for Mercedes.

38 AUSTIN, 1908, Great Britain

After he left the Wolseley company in 1905, Herbert Austin formed his own company at Longbridge, Birmingham, and from 1906 onwards turned out conventional medium- or large-sized touring cars. For the first two years he avoided competitions and concentrated on establishing production and sales of his new product, but a man who had driven in Paris–Vienna and had designed several advanced racing cars (20) could not keep out of sport for long. In 1908 he built four cars for the Grand Prix. They had 9·6-litre, six-cylinder engines rated at 100 h.p., two with chain drive and one driving by shaft. Their engines were the second smallest of any in the race, and one of the drivers, J. T. C. Moore-Brabazon, said that they were not really racing cars at all but very fast tourers. His own shaft-driven car was in fact the first Austin to finish, in eighteenth place. Dario Resta's chain-drive car was nineteenth, while Warwick Wright's car retired on the fifth lap. The cars were not raced again. One survives today in the hands of the Austin Motor Company.

39 MARTINI, 1908, Switzerland

After their conventional Kaiserpreis cars (33), the Martini company built some advanced little machines for the 1908

voiturette races. These had four-cylinder monobloc engines of 1086 cc., with overhead valves operated by a single overhead camshaft, and shaft drive. The cars were entered in the Grand Prix des Voiturettes at Dieppe. Beck's was the fastest of the four-cylinder cars at the beginning of the race, and was well up among the leaders. Unfortunately he fell back later and finished only tenth, while his two team-mates retired. The little Martinis did better in the Coupe des Voiturettes held near Compiègne later in the year. Again three cars were entered, driven by Beck, Richard, and Sonvico. Although two-cylinder cars led the race and occupied the first six places, the Martinis finished first (Sonvico), second (Beck), and fourth (Richard) in the four-cylinder class. The team won the Coupe de Régularité and the Prix Delage for the best-placed 'touring cars'; although hardly everyone's idea of a tourer, the Martinis were probably more suitable for this than most of their rivals. Sonvico also won the Coupe Grégoire for the fastest four-cylinder car in the race. The little overhead camshaft cars were catalogued for two seasons, and three survive today in Switzerland.

40 THOMAS, 1908, U.S.A.

The Thomas was one of the highest-quality American touring cars of the pre-1914 period. It is best remembered for the remarkable victory in the 1908 New York–Paris race, when Montague Roberts and George Schuster drove a 72-h.p., six-cylinder car over 12,116 miles of atrocious roads in 170 days. However, Thomas also went in for racing, building a 60-h.p., six-cylinder car for the 1905 Vanderbilt Cup Eliminating Trials. It had a long bonnet, and the driver, Montague Roberts, sat behind the rear axle. It finished fifth in the Trials, and was not chosen to represent America in the race. Thomas built three cars for the 1906 Vanderbilt Cup, and Roberts was joined by two French drivers, Caillois and Le Blon. The latter qualified for the race and finished eighth. In 1908 the Thomas company decided to enter European racing, and took one car to the Grand Prix, to be driven by Lewis Strang, a nephew of Walter Christie (28). They were the only company to field fewer than two cars (most had three) and the only American competitors. The car (illustrated) had a four-cylinder engine of 11,321-cc. capacity and chain drive, and came into the 'very fast tourer' category in which Moore-Brabazon had placed the Austin (38) rather than a racing car proper. Strang lost first and second gears soon after the start, and retired on the fifth lap with clutch trouble. Three cars of Grand Prix type ran in the 1908 Vanderbilt Cup, and George Salzmann finished fourth. There were no significant sporting entries by Thomas after 1908, but the firm continued to make expensive high-quality tourers until 1913.

41 OPEL, 1908, Germany

After the *débâcle* of the Opel-Darracqs (27) in the 1904 Gordon Bennett Race, the German company avoided first-class racing for several years. However, they developed their touring cars and ran three cars in the 1907 Kaiserpreis,

finishing third and fourth. Encouraged by this success, Opel prepared three cars for the 1908 Grand Prix. They were still touring cars basically, but were naturally larger than any catalogued model, at just over 12 litres. The drivers were Fritz Opel, Carl Joerns, and Michel. Joerns finished sixth, Opel twenty-first, and Michel retired with a burst radiator. It was by no means a discouraging performance, and had Grand Prix racing continued under similar rules for 1909 and 1910, the Opels might have been developed into really competitive machines. However, there was no Grand Prix racing for four years, and when Opel returned in 1913, it was with a much smaller car of totally different design.

42 HUTTON, 1908, Great Britain

The regulations for the 1908 Tourist Trophy Race specified the use of a four-cylinder engine of not more than 4-in. cylinder bore; hence its name of the 'Four Inch Race'. S. F. Edge of Napiers wanted to enter a car for this event, but was reluctant to call it a Napier because he had spent so much energy as an advocate of the six-cylinder engine. Consequently he 'borrowed' the name of J. E. Hutton, an importer of foreign cars who had built a few cars under his own name from 1900 onwards. He was supposed to be building a car with variable-gear transmission for the 1904 Gordon Bennett Race, but it never appeared. The Huttons were made at the Napier works at Acton, London, and followed Napier design closely, with four-speed all-indirect gear-box, detachable wire wheels, and the typical Napier water tower above the radiator. Three cars were entered in the TT, those of Watson and Stirling having 101 × 178-mm. engines, while the car driven by Hutton himself had a 204-mm. stroke. Watson won the race from Algernon Lee Guinness' Darracq, but neither of his team-mates finished the course. Shortly after this Hutton closed down his retail agency and joined the Wolseley company, so he was unable to sell the production Huttons that had been promised by Edge. However, it is by no means certain that Edge had any intention of making four-cylinder Huttons for sale. The long-stroke car took 26-h.p. class records at Brooklands in 1908, and Watson's car ran for several years in sprints and hill-climbs in the North of England.

43 DE DION BOUTON,
1908, France

After the Paris–Madrid De Dion Boutons of 1903 (16), there was a hiatus of several years when the name was not widely known in motor racing. They entered three single-cylinder *voiturettes* in the first Coupe de *l'Auto* of 1905, which was a five-day reliability trial combined with a speed event. De Dion did well in this event, taking first, third, and fifth places, but this was nullified by the subsequent cancellation of the whole event by the Automobile Club de France, so that De Dion and others were forbidden to advertise their successes, and were actually fined for doing so. They did not support the 1906 Coupe des Voiturettes, but several single-cylinder cars appeared in the

1907 Sicilian Cup, a *voiturette* event organized by Cav. Vincenzo Florio, who had also promoted the Coppa Florio and Targa Florio for larger cars. Florio himself was second and two other De Dions were third and fourth. In 1908 no less than seven De Dions ran in the Sicilian Cup, all but one being two-cylinder machines. They were mostly standard touring two-seaters which had been modified for racing by the familiar expedients of lowering the seats, raking the steering columns and removing all road equipment. These cars did well against professionally-prepared racing cars from Sizaire-Naudin and Lion-Peugeot, and the De Dions finished second, third, fourth, and fifth. They did not support the Grand Prix des Voiturettes in 1907 or 1908, although many of the competitors in these races used De Dion engines, and apart from private entries in the 1909 Sicilian Cup and Catalan Cup, the De Dion *voiturettes* were seen no more in racing. However, a small number of sporting two-seaters with single-cylinder engine were sold to the public, and it is one of these that is illustrated. They developed 18 b.h.p. at 2200 r.p.m., giving a maximum speed of about 50 m.p.h.

44 ISOTTA-FRASCHINI,
1908, Italy

Isotta-Fraschini was one of the earliest motor manufacturers in Italy, turning out their first cars in 1899. These were closely based on the French Renault, but from 1905 onwards Isottas were designed by Giustino Cattaneo, a fine engineer who was responsible for the firm's designs up to the 1930s. Most of

Cattaneo's designs were large cars with chain drive, incorporating the advanced feature of a single overhead camshaft. In 1908 there appeared a totally different Isotta, a small car with monobloc four-cylinder engine of only 1327-cc. capacity, also with overhead camshaft. The engine speed was as high as 3500 r.p.m., a remarkable figure when most Grand Prix engines turned at less than 2000 r.p.m. It has been claimed that Ettore Bugatti had a hand in the design of this car, the evidence being that he had been associated with De Dietrich who had a controlling interest in Isotta-Fraschini in 1908, and that his light car of 1909 (51) had striking similarities to the Italian car. However, he had in fact left De Dietrich in 1904, and was working for the German firm of Deutz in 1908. Cattaneo himself denied the Bugatti connection, and it is more likely that Ettore Bugatti examined the Isotta closely at some time, and when he built his own light car a year or so later he incorporated some features of the Italian machine. Three Isotta *voiturettes* (illustrated) were entered in the 1908 Grand Prix des Voiturettes, driven by Trucco, Buzio, and Carlo Maserati, one of the five brothers who later produced racing cars under their own name. Their best result was Buzio's eighth place, but his was the first of the four-cylinder cars at a time when singles and twins dominated *voiturette* racing. This was the only important racing appearance of these advanced little cars, although they were put into limited production and remained in the Isotta-Fraschini catalogue at least until 1910. A few came to England, where they sold for only £285, and one survives in Australia to the present day.

45 VAUXHALL, 1909, Great Britain

The ancestor of all sports Vauxhalls was the staid-looking 16/20-h.p. tourer designed by Laurence Pomeroy which won its class in the 1908 RAC 2000 miles trial. It was remarkably reliable despite an engine speed of 2500 r.p.m., a very high figure for that time, and after the trial its driver Percy Kidner took it to a number of hill-climbs in England and France. In August 1909 Kidner and A. J. Hancock drove two stripped 20-h.p. chassis in the O'Gorman Trophy Race for 20-h.p. cars at Brooklands, and came first and second. By now the engine had been tuned to give 52·6 compared with 38 h.p. for the original 1908 tourer. The next step was to fit a streamlined body, one of the first to appear at Brooklands. It was exceptionally narrow, the radiator cowl tapering to an opening of 16 × 2½ in., while the body was hardly any wider than the driver's shoulders. With an engine now developing over 60 h.p. at 2800 r.p.m., it was expected to have a 'hot' performance, and so was named KN after Cayenne pepper. In December 1909 it established a record for the half-mile at 88·6 m.p.h., and later Hancock covered ten laps at 81·33 m.p.h., which was an improvement on the 40-h.p. record. Later in the same month KN won a match against a 20-h.p. Star, lapping at 76·1 m.p.h. In 1910 Hancock won the O'Gorman Trophy again, and later drove KN, now with a modified body with shorter nose cowl, at over 100 m.p.h. over the flying kilometre. This was the first time that a 20-h.p. car had exceeded the magic 100 m.p.h. figure. Other streamlined record cars were built using the smaller 16-h.p. engine as well as the 20 h.p. In November 1912 Hancock covered 50 miles at an average speed of 97·15 m.p.h. with the 20-h.p. car. This engine was used in the first of the Prince Henry-type sporting tourers which gained many successes in the Swedish and Russian Trials, and which has rightly been considered as one of the world's first true production sports cars.

46 LION-PEUGEOT, 1910,
France

In addition to making motor-cars, the famous Peugeot company produced coffee mills, umbrellas, corsets, and bicycles. Motor-cycles were added to the range in 1903, and it was in the motor-cycle factory at Valentigney, managed by Robert Peugeot, that production began in 1906 of the Lion-Peugeot, at first a single-cylinder chain-driven light car cheaper than any of the Peugeots proper (which were made at Audincourt). Single-cylinder racing *voiturettes* were third in the 1906 and 1907 Coupe de *l'Auto*. These had fairly conventional bore-stroke ratios, but with the restriction on cylinder bore in *voiturette* racing came the famous ultra-long-stroke Lion-Peugeots. The 1908 cars had dimensions of 100 × 170 mm. and a fairly low appearance, but in 1909 came the towering bonnet with two sizes of engine, a 100 × 250 mm. single and a 80 × 192 mm. vee-twin. These were both successful cars, Jules Goux winning the Catalan Cup (single) and Sicilian Cup (twin), and Guippone the Coupe des Voiturettes (single). The singles also did well in hill-climbs, winning the *voiturette* class at Gaillon in

1909 and Mont Ventoux in 1910. The chief racing Lion-Peugeot of 1910 was the VX-5 (illustrated), a vee-twin with dimensions of 80 × 280 mm. The resulting bonnet was so high that driver and mechanic had to peer round rather than look over it, and it had the appearance of being very unstable on corners. Maximum speed was 95 m.p.h. The VX-5 won the Sicilian Cup (Georges Boillot) and Catalan Cup (Goux), and Goux came second in the Coupe des Voiturettes. Another Lion-Peugeot, with four-cylinder engine of 65 × 260 mm. (3440 cc.) was driven into fourth place by Boillot. Lion-Peugeot's last racing season was 1911, when three four-cylinder cars of 78 × 156 mm. (2982 cc.) ran in the Coupe de *l'Auto*, also known as the Coupe des Voitures Légères. Boillot finished second. He might have won had it not been for tire trouble, and it has been suggested that the high build of the Lion-Peugeots placed greater strain on the tires than the lower Delage (52) which won. There were a number of hill-climb successes for the old Lion-Peugeots in 1911, and a VX-5 took some class records at Brooklands, but their racing career was over. The name appeared in 1912 on the 3-litre cars which ran in the Coupe de *l'Auto*, but these had in-line four-cylinder engines and shaft drive. They were the precursors of a new and highly successful line of Peugeots (65), and only in name were they linked with the idiosyncratic long-stroke cars.

47 HISPANO-SUIZA, 1910,
Spain

The first important international motor race in Spain was that for the 1909

Catalan Cup, sponsored by King Alfonso XIII. For this event Marc Birkigt, chief engineer of Hispano-Suiza, who were Spain's leading car manufacturers, designed a four-cylinder monobloc 'T'-head *voiturette* of 1802 cc. The three cars entered did not distinguish themselves on their first outing, two cars retiring and the third finishing last. In the more important Coupe des Voiturettes at Boulogne the Hispano-Suizas finished fifth, sixth, and seventh, and they also won their class at the Monte Igueldo and Mont Ventoux hill-climbs. For the 1910 Catalan Cup cars, Birkigt lengthened the stroke to 170 mm.; Paul Zucarelli finished third behind two Lion-Peugeots. Deciding that more power was necessary, Birkigt lengthened the stroke still further to 200 mm. in the Coupe des Voiturettes cars (illustrated). Capacity was now 2655 cc. and maximum output 60 b.h.p. For the first time on Hispanos, Rudge-Whitworth detachable wire wheels were used. The drivers were Jean Chassagne, a newcomer to the Hispano team, Paul Zucarelli, and L. Pilliverdier. For the first time the tables were turned on the two-cylinder Lion-Peugeots: Zucarelli won at an average speed of 55·6 m.p.h. for the 282 miles, Chassagne was third, and Pilliverdier sixth. The engine of this car was the basis of the 80 × 180 mm., 3·6-litre 'Alfonso'-model Hispano-Suiza, a production sports car made both in Spain and in Hispano's new French factory at Bois-Colombes. The firm did not race in 1911, but in 1912 planned a new 3-litre, four-cylinder car with supercharged single overhead camshaft engine. Because of supercharger troubles they never started in the Coupe de *l'Auto*, although a few were made with narrow tandem-seating two-seater bodywork, and were known as 'Sardines'. The last appearance of the long-stroke 'T'-head Hispano-Suiza was in the 1912 Grand Prix de France, when Rivierre drove a vee-radiator car with 69 × 200 mm. engine. This was probably a 1910 Coupe des Voiturettes engine bored out from 65 to 69 mm. It finished eighth.

48 SUNBEAM, 1911, Great Britain

In 1909 the French engineer Louis Coatalen joined Sunbeam from the Hillman company, and soon produced two new designs, the 12/16-h.p. and 16/20 h.p. four-cylinder 'T'-head-engined cars. He then turned his attention to Brooklands and to the new streamlined cars such as the Vauxhall KN (45), which were being built for the track. Coatalen's first Brooklands car was built during the winter of 1909–10, and was called 'Nautilus'. It had a 92 × 160 mm. (4244-cc.), four-cylinder engine with four overhead valves per cylinder set vertically in the head and operated by two camshafts mounted low down on each side of the crankcase. Thus it still retained features of a 'T'-head layout. The single-seater body consisted of wooden slats fitted on to hoops in the manner of a barrel, and there was a pointed nose cone of brass (which in fact caused overheating). Final drive was by chains, making 'Nautilus' the only chain-driven Sunbeam ever to race at Brooklands. The car was not a great success, but Coatalen was determined to persevere with overhead valves, and in 1911 he produced a new design known as 'Toodles II' (illustrated). This had a shorter-stroke engine of 80 × 160 mm. (3215 cc.), with single overhead camshaft driven by chain and operating inclined overhead valves through rocking levers. The compression ratio was 5:1, a high figure for that time. There was a narrow single-seater body, but much more conventional in appearance than that of 'Nautilus', with a tall vee-radiator in front. 'Toodles' proved a much more successful car than 'Nautilus', and took many records at Brooklands during 1911. These included short ($\frac{1}{4}$-mile) and long (10-lap) class records, the former at 86·16 m.p.h. and the latter at 79·29 m.p.h., as well as some race successes. The latter included Coatalen's victory over a 60-h.p. Napier. A modified version of 'Toodles'' engine with gear-driven overhead camshaft was made in 1912, but does not seem to have been raced, possibly because of Sunbeam's preoccupation with the side-valve cars they were building for the Coupe de l'Auto (64).

49 AUSTIN, 1911, Great Britain

The car illustrated, 'Pearley III', was Austin's answer to the streamlined Brooklands cars such as Vauxhall's KN (45) and Coatalen's Sunbeams (48). It used a standard Austin Twenty engine but with larger valves, lightweight pistons, and a special induction manifold. The body was a streamlined single-seater, though not so freakish in appearance as that of the Sunbeam 'Nautilus' or Vauxhall KN. Disc wheels were used, with Dunlop tires at the front and

Continentals at the rear. In its original 1911 form the engine developed 62 b.h.p. at 2000 r.p.m. During the 1911 season, 'Pearley', driven by Percy Lambert, improved its speed considerably, lapping at 77 m.p.h. on its first appearance at Brooklands and at over 90 m.p.h. by the end of the season. During 1911 Lambert took six thirds and one second place. In October 1911 he took the flying kilometre record in the 21-h.p. class at 93·79 m.p.h. and the flying mile at 91·09 m.p.h. These records lasted for only two weeks until Witchell's Straker-Squire improved on them. During 1912 two Solex carburettors were fitted to 'Pearley', which won several handicap races. Towards the end of 1912 Lambert began to drive the $4\frac{1}{2}$-litre Talbot with which he achieved lasting fame the following year by covering over 100 miles in the hour. This car was designed by G. W. A. Brown, who was also responsible for the Austin Twenties. 'Pearley' survived until at least 1930.

50 BENZ, 1911, Germany

The 200-h.p., four-cylinder Benz, often known as the 'Blitzen' (Lightning) model, first appeared at the Brussels World Championship speed meeting in October 1909. It had a $21\frac{1}{2}$-litre overhead valve engine, cowled radiator, and chain drive. On its first appearance Victor Hémery covered the mile in 31·2 seconds, equal to nearly 120 m.p.h., and the motoring world soon realized that here was a formidable contender for records and hill-climbs, although its engine was too large to be eligible for any existing races. Hémery brought the car to Brooklands in November 1909, and took a number of world records for the standing-start and flying-start half-mile and mile, covering the half-mile at 127·88 m.p.h. and the kilometre at 125·95 m.p.h., the latter being a new World's Land Speed Record. The mile and kilometre records were unbroken, as far as Brooklands was concerned, until after the First World War. In the winter of 1909 Barney Oldfield had a Blitzen Benz shipped to America, where he covered the mile in 27·3 seconds (131·72 m.p.h.), a new record. In 1911 Bob Burman raised this figure to 142·50 m.p.h., but this was not recognized as an official record. The big Benzes had many successes in hill-climbs in France and Germany, leading drivers being Otto Heim and Fritz Erle. The English Benz exponent L. G. Hornsted owned three cars between 1912 and 1914, a 5·7-litre, 27 h.p., a 15-litre car which was similar to the Blitzen but with a bore of 155 mm. compared with the larger car's 185 mm., and the Blitzen itself. With the latter he took twenty-seven world records, many for the standing start, for the big Benz had excellent acceleration, and he also won three races at Ostend in July 1914. The Blitzen was catalogued in 1912 and 1913, and a four-seater was used as a staff car by Field-Marshal von Hinden-berg during the First World War. Several of the cars reappeared at Brook-lands after the war, and a four-seater was driven by Sir Alistair Miller at the track as late as 1930. At least two Blitzens survive, the four-seater afore-mentioned which is in the Birmingham Museum of Science & Industry, and one in the Daimler-Benz museum at Unterturkheim.

51 BUGATTI, 1911, Germany

Ettore Bugatti built the prototype of his light car in the cellar of his home in Cologne, while he was working for the Deutz Gasmotorenfabrik AG (which made large touring cars). This was in the winter of 1908–9, and by the end of 1909 he had found a backer, the banker de Vizcaya, who enabled him to go into small-scale production in a dis-used dyeworks at Molsheim, Alsace. The car had a very neat four-cylinder monobloc engine of 1327 cc. (the proto-type was 1208 cc.), with a single over-head camshaft. From the beginning Bugatti used the banana-shaped curved tappets which were a feature of his de-signs for many years. The little Bugatti was known as the Type 13, being pre-sumably Ettore's thirteenth design, although it is not possible to enumerate all his early designs from 1898 onwards. Five cars were built in 1910 and seventy-five in 1911, the year that the Type 13's sporting career began. The first event entered was the Monte Carlo Rally, held that year for the first time, and this was followed by a hill-climb at Limonest in May, when a Type 13 was second. The first race victories came in June 1911, when Gilbert and de Vizcaya won two events on the Sarthe circuit near Le Mans. Much more important was the Grand Prix de France held in July. This event has been called a 'perambulating motor museum' be-cause of the number of old cars taking part, but one that was not old was Ernst Friderich's little Bugatti. This had a 66 × 100 mm. (1368-cc.) engine and wire wheels in place of the artillery types seen on earlier Bugattis. The race was won by Hémery's 10-litre Fiat, but

Friderich took second place as well as the prize for '*petites cylindrées*' cars. The Type 13 gained a number of hill-climb successes in 1911 and 1912, but had little important racing up to 1914. This was largely due to the fact that there were no races for *voiturettes* until the 1913 Cyclecar Grands Prix, and these were restricted to cars of under 1100 cc. Also Ettore Bugatti was keen on expanding production of the Type 13, and sporting activities were concentrated on the 5-litre chain-driven car which Bugatti drove in hill-climbs and Friderich (in shaft-drive form) at Indianapolis in 1914. However, a team of Type 13s with sixteen-valve engines was prepared for the 1914 Coupe de *l'Auto* race, which was cancelled because of the war. These cars, hidden during hostilities, ran in the 1920 Grand Prix des Voiturettes at Le Mans. Friderich won, and his team-mate Baccoli was fifth. Similar cars finished first, second, third, and fourth in the *voiturette* race at Brescia in 1921, giving rise to the name Brescia for all subsequent short-chassis Type 13 cars, which were made until 1926.

52 DELAGE, 1911, France

The first competition cars made by Louis Delage used De Dion single- or two-cylinder engines, and had a number of successes in *voiturette* racing between 1906 and 1908. The car illustrated, built for the 1911 Coupe de *l'Auto*, was the first racing Delage to use an engine designed and built by the company themselves. It was a 3-litre, long-stroke unit with the familiar dimensions of 80 × 149 mm. The four cylinders were cast in pairs, and the valves were horizontal. Output was

50 b.h.p. at 3000 r.p.m. An unusual feature of the design was the five-speed gear-box with direct drive on fourth, giving an overdrive on top gear. The Coupe de *l'Auto*, or Coupe des Voitures Légères as it was also called in 1911, was held on the Boulogne circuit, an extension giving a longer lap of 32 miles and an increase of over 100 miles in all compared with 1910. Four Delages were entered in the race, driven by Paul Bablot, Albert Guyot, René Thomas, and Victor Rigal. Bablot was hard pressed by Georges Boillot on a Lion-Peugeot (46), but the latter was delayed by tire troubles, and the Delage won at 55·3 m.p.h. Thomas was third and Guyot fourth. The Delages had a number of sprint and hill-climb successes, but were not entered again in a major race. There were no Delages in the 1912 Coupe de *l'Auto*, and the firm's next competition cars were the 6·2-litre cars built for the 1913 Grand Prix (69). One of the 1911 Delages survives today in England.

53 GRÉGOIRE, 1912, France

Founded in 1903, the Grégoire company from Poissy specialized in *voiturettes* as far as racing was concerned, although they did enter a 7·4-litre car for the 1906 Grand Prix. Even this was much smaller than most of its competitors and it made no impression. For the *voiturette* races of 1907 and 1908 the firm made two-cylinder machines of about 1100-cc. capacity, and for the 1911 Coupe de *l'Auto* they built three four-cylinder, 3-litre cars with 'T'-head engines. Like Delage (52) they had overdrive on top gear, though the

Grégoires had only four speeds in all. They did reasonably well, Porporato finishing fifth and de Marne ninth. Unlike Delage, Grégoire were back in the Coupe de *l'Auto* in 1912 with four cars similar to those of 1911, though now with two-speed rear axles giving six speeds in all. The engines were set very far back in the frame so that the radiator was practically in line with the back of the front wheels. This was a possible cause of the steering difficulties which the drivers experienced during the race. Collinet's car crashed on the third lap, and the other Grégoire drivers all withdrew at the end of the first day's racing, saying that the cars were unsafe. They were among the fastest French cars in the event, and their withdrawal was a great disappointment for the French enthusiasts, particularly as the British Sunbeams (64) triumphed on the next day, and the best that France could manage was the fourth place of Croquet's Th. Schneider. The Grégoires were not raced to any great extent again, although Porporato won the 1913 Coupe de la Sarthe. There were no Grégoire entries in the 1913 Coupe de *l'Auto*.

54 ROLLAND-PILAIN, 1912, France

Rolland-Pilain were one of those French regional manufacturers (they came from Tours) who made reliable, high-quality cars for many years, only to be squeezed out of the market by the fatal combination of the Depression and the coming of mass production. Unlike many of their fellows, though, Rolland-Pilain made several sorties into the world of racing, starting in 1908 when

they fielded three four-cylinder, $1\frac{1}{2}$-litre cars in the Coupe des Voiturettes. Their next racing venture was to build two cars for the 1911 Grand Prix de France. Most of the big manufacturers avoided this event, not sponsored by the Automobile Club de France, and there were few new cars built for it. The Rolland-Pilains had 6·1-litre, four-cylinder engines with four valves per cylinder operated by an overhead camshaft, and chain drive. The specification sounded quite promising, but none of the three cars entered finished the course. For the 1912 Grand Prix proper Rolland-Pilain built modified versions of the 1911 cars, now with engines enlarged to 6272 cc. Only two ran, driven by Albert Guyot and a little-known driver called Fauquet who ran under the pseudonym 'Anford'. In fact Anford did better than Guyot, who retired on the second lap with engine trouble. However, when the cars were starting at the beginning of the second day, Monsieur Pilain inadvertently touched Anford's car, so disqualifying the driver and having to take his place. Guyot acted as his mechanic, and they finished ninth. Rolland-Pilain did not support either of the remaining pre-war Grands Prix, and their next appearance in major racing was in 1923 when they entered three cars with twin overhead camshafts and positively closed valves in the Grand Prix. They were not successful.

55 VAUXHALL, 1912, Great Britain

The Coupe de *l'Auto* Vauxhalls were directly descended from the 20-h.p. record car KN (45) and thus from the original Pomeroy-designed 16/20-h.p. tourer of 1908. A single car was entered in the 1911 Coupe de *l'Auto*, driven by A. J. Hancock. It had a standard engine with stroke reduced by 2 mm. to bring it within the 3-litre limit and a curious body with Prince Henry-type radiator, pointed tail, clumsy-looking flared mudguards, and disc wheels. It retired on the third lap with a broken connecting rod. For 1912 Vauxhall returned to the Coupe de *l'Auto* with three cars whose appearance was attractive as the 1911 machine had been ugly. They were low and sleek, with Rudge-Whitworth detachable wire wheels. Output was up to 80 b.h.p. at 3000 r.p.m. from an engine which had produced a bare 38 b.h.p. four years earlier. The drivers were Hancock, Percy Lambert of Austin and Talbot fame, and W. Watson who had driven the 'Four Inch' Hutton (42) in 1908. The Vauxhalls were among the fastest 3-litre cars in the race (which was run concurrently with the Grand Prix, the largest car competing having a capacity of over 15 litres), Hancock making the fastest 3-litre lap on the first day. However they proved more fragile than the Sunbeams, and none of them completed the second day's racing. Two generally similar cars ran in the 1913 Coupe de *l'Auto*, driven by Hancock and Watson, and this time Hancock succeeded in taking fourth place. The 3-litre cars were not raced again, and the only other racing Vauxhalls of the pre-war period were the twin-overhead camshaft cars with hydraulic shock absorbers built for the 1914 Grand Prix and Tourist Trophy. The former used a 100 × 140 mm., 4½-litre engine giving a maximum speed of over 120 m.p.h.,

while the TT cars had capacities of 3·3 litres. Neither model was particularly successful.

56 MATHIS, 1912, Germany

Emile Mathis was a Frenchman living in the Alsatian town of Strasbourg, part of Germany until 1918, so his early cars have to be considered as German. Up to 1911 they were doubly so, for they were designed by the Stoewer company of Stettin and manufactured under licence by Mathis, who added his own hubcaps and radiators. He drove a 3-litre 'Stoewer-Mathis' in the 1911 Coupe de *l'Auto* and finished last, which may have been the reason why his entry for the 1912 race was of his own design. It was by far the smallest car in the race, with a four-cylinder side-valve engine of under 2 litres' capacity. It was also the lightest, but this was its undoing, for the Coupe de *l'Auto* regulations stipulated not only a maximum weight of 900 kg. but a minimum of 800 kg., which rendered the 550 kg. Mathis ineligible for the Coupe. Ironically, there was no minimum weight limit for the concurrent Grand Prix, so the little Mathis was set to run against giants such as the 15-litre Lorraine-Dietrich (60). Driven by Esser, it ran steadily throughout the race, and finished eighth overall. Mathis entered another light car with a slightly larger engine of 2155 cc. in the 1913 Grand Prix, again driven by Esser, but he retired on the ninth lap with engine trouble. The only other Mathis entries in international racing before the war were those of 1057-cc. 'Babylette' light car in the 1913 Cyclecar Grands Prix at Amiens and Le Mans. The faithful Esser was again the driver at Amiens, finishing sixth, while at Le Mans Emile Mathis himself drove again, and finished seventh.

57 ALCYON, 1912, France

Like Grégoire, Alcyon entered motor racing via two-cylinder *voiturettes* in the 1907 and 1908 Grand Prix des Voiturettes and Coupe des Voiturettes. Again like Grégoire, their first four-cylinder racing cars appeared in the 1911 Coupe de *l'Auto*. They were rumoured to have sleeve valves, but when it appeared the sole Alcyon turned out to have inclined overhead valves operated by a single rocker and a push-and-pull rod. Wagner drove it in the Coupe de *l'Auto* but had constant trouble, taking over 1 hour 40 minutes to cover one lap and subsequently retiring. Later in 1911 Barriaux drove the same, or a similar, car in the Grand Prix de France and also retired. For 1912 Alcyon fielded three cars in the Coupe de *l'Auto*, of similar appearance to the 1911 car, with handsome rounded radiator, but with four horizontal valves per cylinder. The drivers were Page, Barriaux, and Arthur Duray, and of these only Duray completed the two days' racing, finishing in sixth place. Barriaux and Duray drove two cars in the 1912 Grand Prix de France, but only the latter finished, ninth and last. Although Alcyons were made until 1928, the marque played no further part in racing.

58 CÔTE, 1912, France

The two-stroke engine has never had a great success in motor racing, although

there have been numerous protagonists of the system, including such illustrious firms as Fiat and Duesenberg. The French manufacturers, Côte of Pantin, Seine, made a series of two- and four-cylinder two-stroke cars from 1908 to 1913, and for two years raced their products without striking success. Three 3-litre, four-cylinder cars ran in the 1911 Coupe de *l'Auto*; two fell out early on with mechanical trouble, but the third, driven by de Vere, finished in tenth place. Like Alcyon, Côte entered three cars in the 1911 Grand Prix de France, but none completed the course. For the 1912 Coupe de *l'Auto* Côte secured the services of the veteran driver Fernand Gabriel, who had won the 1903 Paris–Madrid race on a Mors (7). His team-mate was de Vere. The cars had pair-cast, four-cylinder engines of similar capacity to the previous year's, although they had longer strokes. They wore large, rounded radiators not unlike those of the Alcyons, in place of the flat radiators of 1911. Gabriel retired on the second lap with a broken universal joint, but de Vere went on to finish ninth.

59 CALTHORPE, 1912, Great Britain

A number of British manufacturers supported the 1912 Coupe de *l'Auto*, including Vauxhall, Sunbeam, Singer, and Arrol-Johnston, but none had such a tradition of Continental light car racing as the Birmingham firm of Calthorpe. In 1909 they entered three cars with four-cylinder Alpha engines (the same make that they used in their production cars, although with dimensions reduced to bring them within the regulations), and round radiators. One of the team retired on the first lap, but the other two, driven by Leslie Porter and Fred Burgess, ran steadily, finishing eighth and ninth and winning the Regularity Cup. In 1910 three Calthorpes again were entered in the Coupe de l'*Auto*, with long-stroke engines of their own manufacture and pointed radiators which became a hallmark of racing Calthorpes, though never used on their touring cars. All the cars retired that year, but Calthorpe were back undaunted in 1911, with 2·8-litre engines and four-speed gearboxes in which top was an overdrive. Burgess finished sixth and a Calthorpe was third in a subsequent hill-climb. The 1912 Coupe de l'*Auto* cars (illustrated) were similar in appearance, but had engines with the classic dimensions of 80 × 149 mm., giving 2996 cc. The drivers were Burgess, the French footballer Pierre Garcet, and L. G. Hornsted of Benz fame. Only Garcet survived until the second day, and even he failed to finish. The Calthorpes had one or two hill-climb successes later, but the firm never entered a team in races again. In 1913 they turned their attention to a much smaller car, the 1094-cc. Minor, which was more successful commercially than any of the larger cars. One of these was prepared for Burgess to drive in the 1914 Cyclecar Grand Prix, but this event was cancelled because of the war.

60 LORRAINE-DIETRICH, 1912, France

Lorraine-Dietrich cars were made by the same company who had made the early de Dietrichs (15), the change of name coming in 1906. They supported all three Grands Prix from 1906 to 1908, their best performance being Gabriel's fourth in 1907, and one of the 18-litre 1906 cars was driven by Duray in the 1911 Grand Prix de France. For the 1912 Grand Prix de l'ACF they built four new cars with enormous four-cylinder engines of over 15 litres' capacity. They were the largest cars in the race and, had the makers but realized it, representatives of a dying order, for the 1912 race established that efficient engine design, as represented by the twin-overhead camshaft Peugeots, was of greater effect than sheer size. The four cars were driven by Victor Hémery, Paul Bablot, René Hanriot, and O. Heim. Hémery's car had wire wheels, but the other three had the artillery type and ran with front mudguards in place as if for touring. Hémery made third fastest time on the first lap, passing six cars in the process, but he soon fell out with a cracked cylinder, as did his team-mate Heim. Bablot retired later, and the only member of the team to complete the first day's racing was Hanriot. Even he failed to last out the second day. This disappointing performance was the end of Lorraine-Dietrich as far as Grand Prix racing was concerned, and the firm's next sporting appearance was in sports car racing, when they had several successful years in the 24-hour Le Mans Race in the 1920s. One of the 1912 Grand Prix cars, christened 'Vieux Charles Trois', came to England and ran at Brooklands for many years. As late as 1929 it took Class A records at Brooklands in the hands of the noted old car exponent C. D. Wallbank.

61 STRAKER-SQUIRE,
1912, Great Britain

The Bristol-built Straker-Squire started life in 1906 as the Straker-C.S.B., an English version of the French Cornilleau-Ste. Beuve 25-h.p. touring car. Other models of domestic design followed, but the best and most interesting pre-1914 Straker-Squire was the 3-litre, 15 h.p. of 1910–14 designed by A. H. R. Fedden. This had a four-cylinder side-valve engine which, like that of the 16/20-h.p. Vauxhall (45), was particularly suitable for tuning. The chief exponent of this car at Brooklands was R. S. Witchell, who fitted a streamlined single-seater body to his car which he christened 'PDQ' (Pretty Damn Quick). This particular car (illustrated) had an inlet-over-exhaust engine with one enormous inlet valve in each head and two side-by-side exhaust valves. At the end of 1911 he broke 21-h.p. class records which had been set up two weeks earlier by Pery Lambert's Austin 'Pearley III' (49), and in 1912 he took standing-start records for 10 laps in the course of the O'Gorman Trophy race. He later captured flying start records as well, improving on the existing figures set up by a Singer by over 10 m.p.h. He covered the half-mile at 96·62 m.p.h. Four carburettors were tried on 'PDQ' in 1913, but it proved difficult to synchronize them and they were never used in racing. In addition to its Brooklands achievements the Straker-Squire did well in hill-climbs, winning its class at Aston Clinton, Caerphilly, Pateley Bridge, and Saltburn speed trials. For the 1914 Tourist Trophy Straker-Squire prepared two cars with engines enlarged to 3·3 litres. An overhead camshaft was tried on one in practice but was not used in the race, in which Witchell finished fourth. The 15 h.p. was sold to the public in sporting form, being one of the select band of pre-war British sports cars.

62 SIZAIRE-NAUDIN, 1912, France

The Sizaire-Naudin was one of the most successful racing *voiturettes* of the 1906–8 period, and was also sold in quite large numbers to the public. The first model appeared in 1905, and had the characteristics which distinguished the make for most of its lifetime. These included independent front suspension by sliding pillars and a transverse leaf spring, and direct drive on all three forward speeds, a movable ring on the propeller shaft engaging different sets of teeth on the final drive. It also had an armoured wood frame and was powered by a 918-cc. single-cylinder engine. Georges Sizaire won the 1906 Coupe des Voiturettes, and later successes included first and second places in the 1907 and 1908 Coupe des Voiturettes, first in the 1907 Sicilian Cup, and second in the 1908 Grand Prix des Voiturettes and 1909 Catalan Cup. All these victories were obtained with single-cylinder machines, the largest of which were the 1908 Coupe des Voiturettes cars. These had engines of 100 × 250 mm. (1963 cc.) which developed 42 b.h.p. After 1909 single-cylinder cars could no longer hope to win major *voiturette* races, and Sizaire-Naudin abstained from racing in 1910 and 1911. For the 1912 Coupe de *l'Auto* they fielded three four-cylinder cars (illustrated) with 3-litre engines having four horizontal valves per cylinder. They were supposed to have rotary superchargers 'to assure the complete filling of the cylinders in spite of the enormous speed at which the engine turns', as journalist Charles Faroux remarked. However, these superchargers were not seen when the cars actually turned up at the start. They had the familiar transverse leaf suspension, and held the road well. However, they were underpowered, and none of the three, driven by Georges Sizaire, Louis Naudin, and Robert Schweitzer, finished the race. Even so, they, like their single-cylinder predecessors, had many successes in hill-climbs. They did not appear in the 1913 Coupe de l'Auto, and when the name was next seen in racing, it was on some conventional Ballot-engined light cars which ran in the 1920 Coupe des Voiturettes.

63 EXCELSIOR, 1912, Belgium

The Excelsior company of Saventhem is best remembered for its Albert I luxury touring cars of the 1920s, which were themselves raced in touring car events such as the Spa 24-hour Race. However, the firm made two attempts at the Grand Prix before the war, in 1912 and 1913. For the first year they built a large car with, unusually for a racing car of the period, a six-cylinder engine. Capacity was over 9 litres, making it one of the giants of the race, and at a weight of 1600 kg., the Excelsior was as heavy as the largest car in the event, the 15-litre Lorraine-

Dietrich (60). Another unusual feature was a five-speed gear-box. Driven by Joseph Christiaens, the bright yellow Excelsior had a steady, unspectacular race and finished sixth. The firm were back the following year with two smaller cars, still with six cylinders but of 6107 cc., and a four-speed gear-box. The drivers were Christiaens and L. G. Hornsted, both of whom suffered from the short exhaust stubs, so that they resembled chimney sweeps before the race was half-way through. The cars suffered from plug trouble, and finished no higher than eighth (Christiaens) and tenth (Hornsted). They ran again in the Grand Prix de France, but failed to distinguish themselves. Christiaens took a 1913 car to Indianapolis in 1914, and finished sixth in the 500 Miles Race.

64 SUNBEAM, 1912, Great Britain

Louis Coatalen had built record-breaking cars (48) soon after joining Sunbeams, but he did not venture into international racing until 1911, when a 3-litre car was entered for the Coupe de l'Auto. Despite his experience with overhead valves in his record cars 'Nautilus' and 'Toodles II', Coatalen chose side valves for the racing car on the grounds of greater reliability. The chassis was similar to that of the production 16-h.p. Sunbeam with an identical wheelbase of 9 ft., but the body was an unusual shape, with steeply sloping bonnet and an even steeper slope to the pointed tail. This was said to have been the result of testing at Brooklands. Bolt-on wire wheels were used. The sole car entered, driven by

Richards, retired with broken steering on the eighth lap. For 1912 Coatalen designed a new car with similar-sized engine having larger valves, stronger valve springs and new, lightened connecting rods. This developed 73·7 b.h.p. at 2700 r.p.m., compared with 58 b.h.p. from the 1911 engine. Triou friction-type shock absorbers were fitted, and the wheelbase was shorter than on the production cars. Five of these cars were prepared for the Coupe de l'Auto, four for the race and one spare. The drivers were Victor Rigal, Dario Resta, Gustave Caillois, and Emile Médinger. With the Vauxhalls (55) the Sunbeams proved the fastest cars in the race, and although Caillois retired on the first day, the other three cars finished first, second, and third, driven by Rigal, Resta, and Médinger respectively. Not only did they win the Coupe de l'Auto, but they were only defeated by a 7·6-litre Peugeot and a 14·1-litre Fiat in the Grand Prix itself, which was run concurrently. These 3-litre Sunbeams later had many successes at Brooklands in record-breaking, taking among others the mile class record at 99·45 m.p.h. They also did well in hill-climbs. For 1913 Sunbeam again entered three cars in the Coupe de l'Auto. Their cowled radiators gave them a different appearance from the 1912 cars, and they were advertised as being new machines, but apart from stiffer crankshafts to cope with greater power of 87 b.h.p. at 3000 r.p.m., they were similar to their predecessors. Their best result was Kenelm Lee Guinness' third place. Sunbeam also ran a team of three 4½-litre cars in the 1913 Grand Prix, which was no longer run at the same time as the Coupe de l'Auto.

Chassagne and Resta finished third and sixth. One of the 1912 Coupe de l'Auto cars, the reserve, survives today in the Montagu Motor Museum, Beaulieu, Hampshire.

65 PEUGEOT, 1912, France

Although Peugeot had entered cars in the earliest town-to-town races, they lost interest after about 1900, and the name was only kept alive in sporting circles by the Lion-Peugeot voiturettes (46) made by the Valentigney branch of the firm. However, by 1911 it was obvious that the vee-four Lion-Peugeots were no longer competitive, and something new was needed if the firm were to remain in the racing world. At this time Paul Zucarelli joined Peugeot from Hispano-Suiza, not only as a driver and a very good one, but as a designer also. He and another driver, Jules Goux, were joined by a young Swiss, Ernest Henry, who was originally employed as a draughtsman but soon became a fully-fledged member of the design team. It is impossible to say who was the leader of the team, if it had a leader, but the cars they produced were among the most significant in the history of motor racing. Two designs emerged for the 1912 season, a 3-litre for the Coupe de l'Auto which ran under the name Lion-Peugeot, and a 7·6-litre Grand Prix car (illustrated). Both had the basic characteristics which made these Peugeots so important: twin overhead camshafts operating four inclined overhead valves per cylinder in a hemispherical combustion chamber, central plug location, and all four cylinders cast in one block. Maximum output of the Grand Prix engine was 130 b.h.p. at 2200 r.p.m. The Coupe de *l'Auto* car driven by René Thomas was disappointing, never getting above sixth place and retiring before the end of the first day. However, the Grand Prix car atoned for this in a magnificent victory by Georges Boillot in which he defeated a Fiat (66) with nearly double the engine capacity. Admittedly his teammates Goux and Zuccarelli both retired, and it is a blessing for the history of motor racing that Boillot did not do likewise, for in that case Robert Peugeot might have denied the team further support. As it was, they followed up the Grand Prix success with victories by Goux in the Coupe de la Sarthe and in the 1913 Indianapolis 500 Miles Race.

The 1913 Grand Prix cars were smaller at 5654 cc., but gave little less power at 115 b.h.p., and with them Boillot and Goux scored a 1-2 victory in the Grand Prix, this being the first occasion in the history of the event when one make took the first two places. To back up this success the 3-litre cars dominated the Coupe de *l'Auto*, Boillot finishing first, Goux second, and Rigal fourth. These cars had their valves inclined at an angle of 60° instead of the 45° of the Grand Prix cars, and this greater angle was adopted for all the racing Peugeots from 1914 onwards. One of the 3-litre cars driven by Duray finished second in the 1914 Indianapolis 500 Miles Race, *ahead* of two Grand Prix Peugeots, and it has been suggested that if the 3-litre cars had run in the 1913 Grand Prix they might well have won it. The 1914 Grand Prix was run to a $4\frac{1}{2}$-litre capacity limit, and Henry produced a

4·4-litre car giving 112 b.h.p., or 24·8 b.h.p. per litre. This compares with 17·1 b.h.p. per litre for the 1912 Grand Prix car. The cars had long pointed tails with the spare wheel mounted vertically, a feature which Goux blamed for difficult road holding. They also had front-wheel brakes for the first time. Boillot led for most of the first eighteen laps, but was then overhauled by Lautenschlager's Mercedes 77, and shortly afterwards retired with a broken valve. Goux was fourth and Rigal seventh. The 1913 and 1914 Grand Prix Peugeots had a long career in American racing while Europe was engaged in the First World War.

66 FIAT, 1912, Italy

Ever since the Gordon Bennett days, Fiat had been associated with really large four-cylinder racing cars, and they did not abandon this approach until after 1912. The earlier cars had had inlet-over-exhaust valve engines, but in 1910 Fiat built an enormous record-breaking car, the 28·3-litre S76, with all-overhead valves operated by an overhead camshaft. For the 1911 Grand Prix de France they entered another single-overhead camshaft car, the $10\frac{1}{2}$-litre S61. Hémery won the race against negligible opposition, and the car later had a long career at Brooklands, winning races up to 1927. It still survives today. Their 1912 Grand Prix car, the S74, was a development of the S61, with 14·1-litre overhead camshaft engine and chain drive. After the Lorraine-Dietrich (60) it had the largest engine of any car in the race. Three were entered, driven by Louis Wagner and two Americans, Ralph de Palma and twenty-two-year-old David Bruce-Brown. The latter made a very fine impression in practice for someone who had never driven on the Dieppe course before, and he led the race throughout the first day. For much of the second day he duelled with Boillot for the lead, then after repairing a broken exhaust pipe which lost him some time, he took on fuel at a non-scheduled stop, and so disqualified himself, although apparently he hoped that officials would excuse him on the grounds of unfamiliarity with the course. Wagner came up to take second place behind Boillot in the results. The Fiats had been serious challengers to the new, smaller Peugeots, but they saw the writing on the wall and built no more chain-driven monsters. Bruce-Brown had won the 1911 American Grand Prize in an S74, but he was tragically killed in practice for the 1912 event. However, the Fiat team continued to race, and were rewarded by first and second places for Caleb Bragg and Barney Oldfield.

67 TALBOT, 1913, Great Britain

The 25/50 h.p., 4½-litre Talbot was introduced in 1910 and was at first thought of as a refined, high-quality touring chassis which might carry open torpedo or limousine bodywork. However, in 1912 Percy Lambert appeared at Brooklands with a streamlined single-seater from which a line of sporting 25-h.p. models was developed. Lambert's car did not differ greatly on the mechanical side from the standard production, but had a larger carburettor, lighter connecting rods and new pistons, and a higher rear axle ratio. The streamlining of the body was quite typical of Brooklands practice at the time, although a refinement was the fairing-over of the front and rear dumb-irons. The engine developed 130 b.h.p. at 3500 r.p.m. On its first outing the car lapped at 109·43 m.p.h. and took the Class F (5-litre) record for the half mile at 113·28 m.p.h. In February 1913 Lambert became the first man in the world to cover over a hundred miles in one hour, which was a very different thing from achieving 100 m.p.h. for a short distance. His first attempt was defeated by tire trouble at the last moment, but on his second, in far from favourable weather, he covered 103·84 miles in the hour. The company issued some interesting statistics in connection with this record, such as that 80 charges of petrol were drawn in, compressed, fired, expanded, and swept out every second, and that at 105 m.p.h. each piston covered 5½ inches each way over 80 times per second. For races in the autumn of 1913 a new engine with 150-mm. stroke, compared with the standard 140 mm. was installed in Lambert's car. This gave a capacity of 4754 cc. In October 1913 Talbot lost the World Hour Record to a 9-litre, vee-twelve Sunbeam driven by Jean Chassagne, and while attempting to regain it Lambert crashed in mysterious circumstances and was killed. It is probable that a rear tire burst when the car was high on the Brooklands banking. As well as Lambert's special car, a number of sporting 25/50s were sold to the public, and made a very good name for themselves in hill-climbs up to the outbreak of war.

68 SCHNEIDER, 1913, France

The Schneider company of Besançon was founded by Théophile Schneider, who had formerly been one of the partners in the Lyons firm Rochet-Schneider. The first Schneiders, or Th. Schneiders as they were sometimes called to distinguish them from the Lyons cars, appeared in 1910 and were characterized by a dashboard radiator. For the 1912 Coupe de *l'Auto* Schneider prepared three cars with special racing engines of 80 × 149 mm. (2996 cc.), but they were not ready in time, and the cars which reached the starting line had standard 15·9-h.p. engines of 80 × 120 mm. (2413 cc.). They were thus at a disadvantage in size compared with the Sunbeams, Peugeot, and other Coupe de *l'Auto* contenders, and in the circumstances Croquet's fourth place was highly creditable. Three Schneiders ran in the 1912 Grand Prix de France, finishing second, fourth, and sixth. Encouraged by these successes the company entered four cars in the 1913 French Grand Prix. This time they used specially-built engines larger than any production Schneiders had. They were 5·5-litre, 'L'-head units with four cylinders cast *en bloc*. The team of four (Croquet, Gabriel, Champoiseau, and René Thomas) was the largest of any make except Sunbeam in what was an exceptionally small field for a Grand Prix anyway: only twenty cars. The Schneiders were not in the class of the leading cars as far as speed was concerned, but they were steady and cornered well. Their best position was Champoiseau in seventh place. The firm ran three cars in the 1914 Grand

Prix, this time with 4·4-litre overhead-valve engines and frontal radiators. Again Champoiseau was their first finisher, in ninth place. One of the 1914 cars made several appearances at Brooklands in the 1920s, but the firm never built racing cars again. Their 2-litre sports cars were, however, seen in events such as the Le Mans 24-hour Race up to 1927.

69 DELAGE, 1913, France

Despite Delage's success with their 1911 Coupe de *l'Auto* cars (52) they had no entries in 1912, either in the Coupe de *l'Auto* or the Grand Prix, but returned to racing in 1913 with a team of the 6·2-litre cars illustrated. They were in many ways similar to the 1911 cars, with four horizontal valves per cylinder and five-speed gear-boxes with overdrive on top. The engine was now a monobloc, compared with the pair-cast unit of 1911. Output was about 130 b.h.p. Two cars ran in the Grand Prix, both driven by experienced men, Paul Bablot and Albert Guyot. The Delages made a very good impression in practice, and were thought to have an equal chance with the Peugeots of Boillot and Goux (65). Guyot was leading for six laps in the middle of the race when a tire burst. His mechanic jumped out, misjudging the speed as many people might do when a car was slowing from 90 m.p.h. or so, fell and was run over by the rear wheel. Guyot changed the tire himself and then drove the injured mechanic to the pits. This lost him sixteen minutes and all chance of victory. He finished fifth, while team-mate Bablot was fourth. Bablot and Guyot came first and second in the less-important Grand Prix de France at Le Mans, while in 1914 two of the Delages ran at Indianapolis in the 500 Miles Race, René Thomas winning at 82·47 m.p.h. For the 1914 Grand Prix Delage produced some very advanced cars with 4½-litre twin-overhead camshaft engines, twin carburettors, and five-speed gear-boxes. However, these proved very disappointing, two of the team retiring with engine trouble, and the third, Duray, finishing no higher than tenth. One of the 1913 Grand Prix cars survives today.

his retirement Moriondo had overturned his car against a protective bank in front of a grandstand. He and his mechanic Jules Foresti managed to set the car back on its wheels after several attempts, changed a front wheel and rejoined the race, to prolonged applause. The Italas were not particularly fast, and even had they not retired they would have had little chance of finishing near the winner. Moriondo's car came to Brooklands in 1914 and, fitted with a single-seater body and radiator cowl, was raced there with some success by Robertson Shersbie-Harvie.

70 ITALA, 1913, Italy

After their 1908 Grand Prix cars (36) Itala took no part in racing until 1913, when they built a team of three cars for the Grand Prix. These had 8·3-litre pair-cast, four-cylinder engines with rotary valves, which Itala were using in their production cars at that time. The Grand Prix cars bore in the corner of their radiators the word 'avalve', meaning valveless, indicating to the spectators that if they were not valveless in the true sense, at least their breathing arrangements were not strictly conventional. The three drivers were the famous Felice Nazzaro, who had made such a name for himself with Fiat, Moriondo, and H. R. Pope, chairman of the British Itala company. Pope was a last-minute addition to the team, replacing Bigio who had been killed in practice together with his mechanic. The team had a disappointing race, Pope retiring on the first lap with a run big-end, while Moriondo and Nazzaro retired with broken rear springs. Before

71 DUESENBERG, 1914, U.S.A.

The German-born Duesenberg brothers began their automotive career building two-cylinder Mason touring cars at Des Moines, Iowa, in 1907. Three years later Fred Duesenberg built his first racing engine, a 5·7-litre, four-cylinder monobloc unit with two horizontal valves per cylinder, operated by large vertical rocker arms. It was from these that the engine derived its name, 'the walking-beam engine'. In its initial form the engine developed about 90 b.h.p., but this was improved to 100 b.h.p. by 1912. Cars fitted with this engine were raced under the Mason name until 1914, and thereafter as Duesenbergs. The Mason company was not particularly interested in racing, and early in 1914 the Duesenbergs moved to St Paul, Minnesota where they rented some space in a large machine shop. Their racing successes had begun earlier when, under the Mason name, they came first and second in the 1912 Wisconsin Trophy race at Milwaukee. They ran at Indianapolis for the first time in 1913, finishing ninth and thirteenth. The first cars to race as Duesenbergs, the 1914 models, had engines enlarged to 5960 cc. giving 120 b.h.p. Eddie Rickenbacker began to drive for the brothers, and finished tenth at Indianapolis. Two months later he won the 300-mile Sioux City race, and another Duesenberg was fifth. The brothers also built a straight-twelve 'walking-beam' engine for marine use, and Commodore J. A. Pugh's *Disturber IV*, fitted with two of these engines, was the first boat to exceed 60 m.p.h. They continued to build racing cars with 'walking-beam' engines in 1915 and 1916, introducing four valves per cylinder in the latter year. Several famous names became associated with these cars, including Ralph Mulford and Tommy Milton. They won in three different types of racing current in America at that time, road events such as the Corona (California) Grand Prize, dirt tracks such as Ascot (Los Angeles), and the new board speedways such as Des Moines, Tacoma, and Cincinnati. Their best performance at Indianapolis was Wilbur d'Alene's second place in 1916, but the Duesenberg name was frequently among the Indianapolis winners in later years (86). There was no racing in 1917 and 1918 because of America's entry in the First World War, and the Duesenbergs were busy making aircraft engines in a new factory at Elizabeth, New Jersey. They built no more racing cars with 'walking-beam' engines, although the layout was used in engines made for sale to other firms such as Biddle, Revere, and Roamer.

72 A.L.F.A., 1914, ALFA-ROMEO, 1921, Italy

The A.L.F.A. company (Sta. Anonima Lombarda Fabbrica Automobili) was formed in 1910 as an outgrowth of a company which had built Darracq light cars under licence. The new products were designed by Giuseppe Merosi, a distinguished engineer who remained with the company until 1924. His cars were straightforward four-cylinder side-valve machines, of which the 4084-cc. 20/30-h.p. model was typical. In its original form the engine developed 42 b.h.p. at 2200 r.p.m. Two ran in the 1911 Targa Florio but retired with engine trouble, though examples driven by Franchini and Campari came third and fourth in the 1913 Coppa Florio. Two other interesting cars were built by A.L.F.A. before the First World War; the 40/60 h.p. with 6082-cc. overhead-valve engine, which had a number of racing and hill-climb successes, and a $4\frac{1}{2}$-litre twin-overhead camshaft car built for the 1914 Grand Prix. Unfortunately this was not ready in time, and did not race until after the war, and then only in national events. During the war the A.L.F.A. company became part of a combine headed by Nicola Romeo, and the 20/30 appeared in 1919 under the name Alfa Romeo. The Type ES sports model now had an engine of 4250 cc. developing 67 b.h.p. at 2600 r.p.m., and a number of competition successes were obtained. Enzo Ferrari was second in the 1920 Targa Florio in a pre-war 20/30, and in 1921 Antonio Ascari and Ugo Sivocci were first and second in their class in the Parma-Berceto hill-climb. Sivocci and Ferrari were fourth and fifth, and won their class, in the 1921 Targa Florio. The 40/60 also appeared in post-war guise and had a number of successes, but both models were overshadowed by the new four-cylinder Merosi design, the 3-litre RL, which appeared in 1922.

73 VIOLET-BOGEY, 1913, France

Marcel Violet was one of the most determined advocates of the two-stroke engine in France, and designed a wide variety of such engines between 1908 and 1948. In 1911 he was a consultant to the Côte company, and certainly had a hand in the four-cylinder two-stroke racing cars entered in the Coupe de l'Auto in 1911 and 1912 (58). A two-cylinder two-stroke engine was tried in his own production, the Violet-Bogey cyclecar, but production versions used a four-stroke overhead inlet-valve unit of 1088 cc. developing 22 b.h.p. at 2400 r.p.m. It had the advanced features, unusual on a cyclecar, of pressure lubrication and a ball-bearing crankshaft. Friction transmission was used, and final drive was by single chain to a differential-less rear axle. Two cars basically similar to the production machines, although with sketchier bodywork, ran in the 1913 Cyclecar Grands Prix, driven by Violet himself and Pouliez. In the first race at Amiens Pouliez finished fourth and Violet, who had been leading at one point, shed a rear wing and was disqualified. In the Le Mans Cyclecar Grand Prix Violet was second. The same chassis, now equipped with a two-stroke engine, appeared in 1920 under the name

Major, and with this car Violet won the Grand Prix des Cyclecars. The two-stroke cars appeared later under the names Mourre and Weler, the former apparently identical to the Major, the latter using the same engine but having conventional transmission and shaft drive. Violet also built the Sima-Violet two-stroke cyclecar between 1924 and 1929, a 1½-litre flat-four Grand Prix car in 1926, and made the engines for Bucciali two- and four-cylinder racing cars of the mid-20s.

74 PICCARD-PICTET, 1914, Switzerland

With Martini (33, 39), Piccard-Pictet was one of the leading Swiss makes of car before the First World War. The first machines to leave their Geneva factory were the straight-eight Dufaux racing cars of 1904 (30), but in 1906 they began production of touring cars, under the name S.A.G. (Societé des Automobiles à Genève) until 1910 and thereafter as Piccard-Pictet or Pic-Pic. From about 1910 onwards they produced a number of competition cars which did well in hill-climbs and speed trials in Switzerland, France, and Spain. In 1912 the company began to make sleeve-valve engines, and their only entry in major international events, the 1914 Grand Prix cars (illustrated), used this system. They had 4½-litre, four-cylinder engines developing 150 b.h.p. at 3000 r.p.m., and four-wheel brakes. This latter feature was also found on Peugeot, Delage, and Fiat (75) cars in this race. In original form the Grand Prix cars had pointed tails, but when they actually appeared at Lyons they had bolster tanks with the spare wheels behind. The drivers were Tournier, who had been a regular driver for the works for several years, and a young Englishman, Thomas Clarke. Sadly, the cars did not do well in the Grand Prix, having neither speed nor reliability. Clarke was last for a number of laps before retiring with engine trouble, while Tournier circulated for seventeen laps before retiring also.

75 FIAT, 1914, Italy

The appearance of the 1914 Grand Prix Fiat heralded a complete change in the company's competition cars. Peugeot's victory in 1912 over the enormous 14·1-litre Fiat S74 demonstrated to the Italians that a well-designed small engine, with consequent saving of weight and gain in handling, was a better proposition than a larger, less efficient engine. They had no entry in the 1913 Grand Prix, but for 1914 built three cars with twin overhead camshafts and four-wheel brakes. The monobloc four-cylinder engines had one inlet and two exhaust valves per cylinder, and developed 130 b.h.p. They had attractive low lines, with side-mounted spare wheels and pointed tails. Of the drivers, only one, Allesandro Cagno, was well-known in Grand Prix racing, and had driven for Itala in 1906 to 1908. The others were Antonio Fagnano and an Englishman, Jack Scales, who drove Chiribiri light cars in the 1920s. Cagno's car was off tune, but both Scales and Fagnano attracted favourable attention. However, Scales retired with a broken camshaft drive and Fagnano, although he was sixth at one point, finished no

higher than eleventh. Later, the engine was enlarged from $4\frac{1}{2}$ litres to 4·9 litres, with the intention of competing at Indianapolis. Fiat never did so with this car, but they had some success in the immediate post-war period. Count Giulio Masetti was third in the 1919 Targa Florio, and won this event in 1921.

76 NAGANT, 1914, Belgium

Nagant Frères of Liège began building cars in 1900, following the Gobron-Brillié opposed-piston principle (14). They were sold as Gobron-Nagants, and took part in a number of early races, including Paris–Vienna and the 1902 Circuit des Ardennes. In the former event they did better than the genuine French Gobron-Brilliés, which were new, untried, front-engined designs. In 1905 Nagant turned to the manufacture of conventional four-cylinder cars, and took little part in sport for a number of years. A new side-valve engine, the 14/16 h.p., appeared in 1911. Like the Vauxhall in England, this engine proved very suitable for tuning, and reawakened the firm's interest in racing. A number of 14/16s, some fitted with streamlined single-seater bodies and disc wheels, ran in Belgian speed events such as the Coupe de la Meuse and the Ostend Speed Weeks. In 1914 the firm decided to enter the field of Grand Prix racing. They built two cars with advanced $4\frac{1}{2}$-litre twin overhead camshaft engines and five-speed gear-boxes. These were driven by Esser and Elskamp in the race. Esser was the faster of the two and finished in sixth place, behind three

Mercedes, a Peugeot, and a Sunbeam. Considering the experience of these firms, Esser's performance was highly creditable. Unfortunately the war interrupted any further Grand Prix ventures that Nagant might have had in mind, and when they returned to competitions, it was with touring cars in the Spa 24-hour Race.

77 MERCEDES, 1914, Germany

In 1913 the Mercedes company showed a revival of interest in racing, and built two new models, a small four-cylinder sleeve-valve Knight-Mercedes which finished fifth at Indianapolis, and a six-cylinder car with overhead camshaft and four valves per cylinder, although it still retained the archaic feature of chain drive. This car ran in the 1913 Grand Prix de France, finishing fourth, and later went to America where Ralph de Palma had a number of successes with it. The engine was to some extent copied in the 4½-litre cars which Mercedes built for the 1914 Grand Prix. These had overhead camshafts operating inclined overhead valves with hemispherical combustion chambers, three sparking plugs per cylinder, and dual magneto ignition. The engine had an old-fashioned look, with exposed valve springs and stems. Final drive was by shaft, but braking was on the rear wheels only. Thus it was by no means the most modern design to line up at Lyons on 4 July 1914, but Mercedes made up for this with the reliability of the cars and the thoroughness of their preparation, testing, and practice. In

this they provided a foretaste of the Alfred Neubauer era of Mercedes-Benz racing in the 1930s. Before going to the circuit they selected six alternative final drive ratios, which would be tested on the spot to determine the most suitable, and took seventy-two axle shafts to Lyons. Five cars were entered (the maximum allowed); Sailer led at the outset in order to break up the Peugeot opposition, but went out on the sixth lap with a broken crankshaft. Boillot's Peugeot led from lap five to lap fifteen, but on an order from the Mercedes pit Lautenschlager, Salzer and Wagner began to move up, Boillot retired on the final lap having been passed by Lautenschlager, and the German cars finished 1-2-3, the order being Lautenschlager, Wagner, Salzer. It was a great triumph for German organization, and a fitting close to pre-war racing in Europe. The Mercedes' career was far from over, however, for one went to America, where Ralph de Palma won the Chicago Cup and Elgin Trophy in 1914, and the Indianapolis 500 Miles Race in 1915. He also won two races in 1916 from a 4½-litre Grand Prix Peugeot driven by Dario Resta. No fewer than three 1914 Mercedes ran in the 1922 Targa Florio, two entered by the works and driven by Lautenschlager and Salzer, and Count Masetti's privately-owned example, which won. All the Targa cars had front wheel brakes. Salzer made fastest time of the day at the Semmering hill-climb in 1924, and as late as 1926 Caracciola repeated this performance, this time using a supercharger on the old Grand Prix car. The last triumph of the 1914 cars seems to have been Rosenberger's fastest time of the day at the Herkules hill-climb in 1927. Three of the cars survive, one in England (Lautenschlager's winning car), one in the Briggs Cunningham Collection at Costa Mesa, California (the reserve car), and one at the Mercedes-Benz museum at Unterturkheim, which is a hybrid of the two works Targa Florio cars.

78 OPEL, 1914, Germany

After their 1908 Grand Prix entries, Opel played little part in racing until the 1913 Grand Prix, when they entered a lone 3·9-litre, four-cylinder car. It had a single overhead camshaft operating valves inclined at 45°, shaft drive, and only three speeds. The driver was Carl Joerns, who had to practise on the Amiens circuit in a touring car as the Grand Prix car was not ready. This is not quite so unusual as it would be today, for over two weeks elapsed between the last practice day and the race itself. In the race Joerns did very badly, bringing up the rear of the field on the first lap, and retiring during the second. For 1914 Opel built three Grand Prix cars with monobloc engines, four-speed gear-boxes, and again, single overhead camshafts. They were driven by Joerns, Erndtmann, and Breckheimer. Their performance was not very exciting, no Opel being higher than fourteenth for the bulk of the race, although last-minute retirements allowed Joerns into tenth place at the finish. His team-mates retired. One of the Grand Prix cars was acquired after the war by Sir Henry Segrave and driven by him at Brooklands in 1920.

79 SUNBEAM, 1914, Great Britain

Up to 1914 Sunbeam's many racing successes had been achieved with side-valve-engined cars which were basically tuned touring cars. However, Coatalen realized that increasingly specialized cars from firms such as Peugeot would inevitably prove superior in the long run, so for 1914 he produced a very close copy of the Peugeot engine for both his Grand Prix and Tourist Trophy (illustrated) cars. The four-cylinder engines had four valves per cylinder, inclined at 60° and operated by twin overhead camshafts. The 3·3-litre Tourist Trophy engines developed 99 b.h.p. at 3000 r.p.m. but ran at up to 3200 r.p.m. during the race. This compares interestingly with the 90 b.h.p. at 2900 r.p.m. developed by the 1913 Coupe de l'Auto Peugeot from 2980 cc. Three Sunbeams were entered in the Tourist Trophy, driven by Dario Resta and Algernon and Kenelm Lee Guinness. With the Vauxhalls they were the lightest cars in the race and were joint favourites. 'KLG' went into the lead on the first lap of the two-day race, and at the end of the first day's racing the Guinness brothers were in first and second places. 'KLG' held first place throughout the second day, winning at 56·44 m.p.h. for the 600-mile event. His brother retired towards the end of the second day with universal joint failure, and Resta had fallen out on the first day through the failure of an experimental type of big-end. The Grand Prix Sunbeams were very similar to the TT cars, although with larger engines of 94 × 160 mm., giving a capacity of 4441 cc. Three cars were entered, the best result being Resta's fifth place. Two of the Tourist Trophy cars survive today in England.

80 STUTZ, 1915, U.S.A.

Harry C. Stutz completed his first car in five weeks and entered it in the 1911 Indianapolis 500 Miles Race. Gil Anderson drove it into eleventh place in a field of thirty-three, earning it the name which became a company slogan: 'The Car That Made Good in a Day'. For the next three years Stutz had many successes, the Bearcat roadster becoming one of America's most famous cars. They used a 6·3-litre 'T'-head engine built for Stutz by the Wisconsin Motor Company, although a six-cylinder Stutz-built engine was also available. Up to 1915 the racing cars used the same engines as the showroom products, but in that year Stutz ordered from Wisconsin a new engine based on European design. It was generally similar to the Mercedes (77) in layout, with single overhead camshaft, four valves per cylinder and exposed valve stems, but it used Peugeot's chain drive for the camshaft. The 4·9-litre engine developed 130 b.h.p. at about 3300 r.p.m. Three of these engines were made, and fitted into cars rather different in appearance from the general run of Stutzes, with tall, narrow radiators, and wire wheels. Known as the 'White Squadron' Stutzes, they ran in all the major American races of 1915, winning at Point Loma, California (Earl Cooper), Minneapolis Speedway (Cooper), and the Elgin Road Race (Gil Anderson). They were also first and second (Anderson and Cooper) at Sheepshead Bay Board Speedway. The Stutz Company won the A.A.A. National Championship for makes in 1915, and their drivers Cooper and Anderson were first and third respectively in the Drivers' National Championship. Successful though they were, the White Squadron Stutzes were really 'one-season cars', for they won no races in 1916 and only one in 1917. They were back at Indianapolis in 1919, when Eddie Hearne did well to finish second. This was the highest position Stutz ever achieved at their home-town speedway.

81 PREMIER, 1916, U.S.A.

The early Indianapolis 500 Miles Races were notable for the number of foreign cars taking part, and while victories by such makes as Peugeot (1913), Delage (1914), and Mercedes (1915) may have injured American pride, they at least stimulated domestic manufacturers and provided exciting racing. The shortage of foreign entrants for the 1916 race, caused by the war, seriously alarmed the organizers, who tried to order some Peugeots from France, to be used by American drivers. When Peugeot replied that they were totally involved in the war effort and could not help, the Speedway Corporation commissioned the local Premier Motor Manufacturing Company to build three replicas of the 1914 Grand Prix Peugeot. The choice of Premier was not simply because of its proximity to the Speedway, but also because Carl G. Fisher of the Speedway Corporation had a high regard for the talents of G. A. Weidely, the Premier designer who had built a single overhead camshaft hemispherical-head engine in 1905. The three Premier-Peugeots, as they were sometimes called, were driven in the race by Howdy Wilcox, Tom Rooney, and Gil Anderson. Wilcox finished seventh, but his team-mates retired. The race was won, incidentally, by a 'genuine' 1914 Peugeot driven by Dario Resta. During practice for the 1919 '500' Jules Goux cracked a cylinder block on his 1914 Peugeot, and this was hastily replaced by a Premier block which enabled Goux to finish third in the race.

82 STRAKER-SQUIRE, 1918, Great Britain

Straker-Squire began work on the design of their post-war car before the end of the First World War, and had two prototypes running on the road in November 1918, the month that hostilities ceased. The car illustrated is the second of these prototypes. The design incorporated six separately-cast cylinders with a single overhead camshaft operating overhead valves via exposed rockers. Capacity was 3·9 litres, and in its original form the engine developed 70 b.h.p. at 2500 r.p.m. Unlike the pre-war Straker-Squires (61) the new car was made in London, not Bristol. In order to test the prototype thoroughly, Sidney Straker lent it to his nephew, H. Kensington Moir, to race at Brooklands and other places. Moir first brought it to the track in September 1920, setting Class F records including the half mile at 99·99 m.p.h. and ten miles at 94·97 m.p.h. He also took the Test Hill record at 25·41 m.p.h. In 1921 Moir fitted a radiator cowl, and later painted the car in dazzling black and

white zig-zag stripes. In this form, and with the engine tuned to give 115 b.h.p., the Straker-Squire won several short races, its fastest lap being 103·76 m.p.h. Not more than sixty of the 3·9-litre Straker-Squires were made, between 1920 and 1925, of which a tourer survives in Australia and the car illustrated in Great Britain.

83 BALLOT, 1919, France

Ernest Ballot was a manufacturer of proprietary engines in Paris who, in 1919, decided that his firm's prestige would be aided by success in the field of motor racing. His own engines were utterly unsuitable for such a purpose, so he engaged the services of Ernest Henry, the Swiss designer who had been a member of the team which created the 1912 Grand Prix Peugeot (65). Henry had little time at his disposal, for it is said that Ballot only made his decision to race on Christmas Eve 1918, and the cars were wanted for Indianapolis at the end of May 1919. Henry followed the pattern of twin overhead camshafts operating inclined overhead valves that he had used on the Peugeot, but the Ballot differed in having eight cylinders in line. Two carburettors were used, and the 4·9-litre engine gave about 130 b.h.p. Four cars were ready by 26 April, having been designed and built in 101 days. The drivers at Indianapolis were Paul Bablot, Albert Guyot, René Thomas, and Louis Wagner. The Ballots were easily the fastest cars at Indianapolis, and Thomas lapped at 104·7 m.p.h., 5 m.p.h. faster than the existing lap record. Unfortunately they were found to be over-geared, and as the team, surprisingly, had no alternative rear axle ratios with them, they had to fit smaller American wheels and tires which gave constant trouble. Their best result was Guyot's fourth place. At one point Bablot overturned, but the car was set on its wheels again and continued the race. Later in the season the Ballots were fitted with front wheel brakes and, so equipped, one ran in the Targa Florio in November 1919. After driving the car the whole way from Paris to Naples, Thomas made second fastest time on the first lap. The twisting circuit and atrocious roads did not give the Ballot any chance to make use of its full power, and after a brave drive Thomas suffered differential failure on the last lap. The 4·9-litre Ballots were not seen again in major events, although they did well in hill-climbs (Thomas had broken the record at Gaillon before the Targa Florio), and one came to Brooklands where Count Louis Zborowski lapped at 112·17 m.p.h.

84 SUNBEAM, 1920, Great Britain

The Sunbeam company had had experience of building aero-engined racing cars before the First World War; a 9-litre vee-twelve had taken a number of records at Brooklands in 1913 and 1914. Shortly after the war Coatalen decided to build a racing and sprint car using the 18-litre Manitou vee-twelve aero engine that the company had developed during the war for use in Royal Naval Air Service seaplanes. This engine had four valves per cylinder and four six-cylinder mag-

netos. It developed 300 b.h.p. at 2000 r.p.m. It was considerably modified for use in the car, with a stroke lengthened by 10 mm. to give a capacity of 18,322 cc., while the four valves per cylinder were replaced by two exhaust and one inlet valve, operated by one overhead camshaft above each bank of cylinders. Two twelve-cylinder magnetos fired two plugs in each cylinder. Two Claudel-Hobson carburettors were used, and the engine now gave 350 b.h.p. at 2000 r.p.m. The car had a four-speed gear-box and shaft drive, the latter an unusual feature in the aero-engine monsters of this date, which mostly used chains. The Sunbeam was altogether a more sophisticated car than its contemporaries such as Zborowski's Chitty-Bang-Bangs (92) or Eldridge's Isotta-Maybach. It first appeared at Brooklands in the summer of 1920, when it crashed, though not seriously. In October 1920 René Thomas set up a new record for the Gaillon hill-climb at over 109 m.p.h. In 1922 Kenelm Lee Guinness set up a number of records a: Brooklands in the Sunbeam, including the flying kilometre at 133·75 m.p.h., which was a new World's Land Speed Record, beating the eight-year-old record set up by Hornsted's Benz, also at Brooklands, by 9 m.p.h. Guinness lapped at 123·39 m.p.h., which was the first time that Brooklands had been officially lapped at more than 120 m.p.h. This occasion was the last time that the World's Land Speed Record was established at Brooklands, but not the last time for the 350 h.p. Sunbeam, which was acquired by Malcolm Campbell in 1925. He improved the streamlining by fitting a longer cowl and tail, and at Pendine Sands in Wales raised the record to 150·86 m.p.h. on 21 July 1925. After the Second World War the car was completely restored to its original Brooklands form by Harold Pratley, and is now on exhibition at the Montagu Motor Museum, Beaulieu, Hampshire.

85 PEUGEOT, 1920, France

After Ernest Henry left Peugeot for Ballot, the Sochaux company engaged Grémillon as their chief engineer. Under his direction a team of 3-litre cars was prepared for the 1920 Indianapolis race. In appearance they were typically Peugeot, looking not unlike the 1914 Grand Prix cars, but under the bonnet there was a most unusual engine sporting three overhead camshafts and five valves per cylinder. Output was 105 b.h.p. at 4000 r.p.m., and the engine was integral with the four-speed gearbox. Four cars went to Indianapolis, three for the race and one reserve. The drivers were Jules Goux, André Boillot, and Howard Wilcox. During practice a number of problems were encountered, but the necessary spare parts arrived too late, having been delayed by a dock strike at Le Havre. The drivers did not have confidence in their cars, and results were disappointing. The best position attained was Wilcox's sixth place for a while, but he fell back, and none of the Peugeots finished in the first ten. The three-camshaft cars were quietly dropped, and for 1921 a more conventional twin overhead camshaft design was produced. Wilcox and Chassagne drove these at Indianapolis, but Chassagne shed his bonnet and had to retire, while Wilcox, though in

second place at one point, suffered a broken connecting rod and also retired. This was the end of Peugeot's major racing activity, although they had some success in the Coppa Florio in the mid-20s.

86 FRONTENAC, 1921, MONROE-FRONTENAC, 1920, U.S.A.

The Frontenac racing cars were designed by Louis Chevrolet and driven by him and his brother Gaston as well as by many of the leading drivers of the day. The make first appeared at Indianapolis in 1916, when three cars were entered. One had a 4·9-litre twin overhead camshaft four-cylinder engine with inclined valves and hemispherical combustion chambers, with a cast-iron head and block, and aluminium crankcase. The other two Frontenacs had single overhead camshaft engines, but made more extensive use of aluminium, in the block and crankcase, inlet manifold, camshaft cover, and pistons. None of these cars completed the 500 miles at Indianapolis, but they had a number of successes later, including Louis Chevrolet's victory at the Uniontown, Pennsylvania Board Speedway in December 1916. The 1920 cars (lower illustration) were built in the factory of the William Small Company, an Indianapolis firm who made the Monroe touring car. The design was Chevrolet's, although he was aided by Cornelius van Ranst, a former Duesenberg engineer. The 3-litre engine was generally similar to the 1916 twin overhead camshaft engine. Magneto ignition was used on the cars in practice, but the winning car at any rate used a Delco coil in the race. No fewer than seven cars were built for the 1920 Indianapolis race, four of which were entered as Monroes and three as Frontenacs. Five retired or crashed with broken steering arms, but Gaston Chevrolet atoned for this by winning at a speed of 88·17 m.p.h. This was the first time that an American car had won the nation's premier race since 1912. For 1921 Chevrolet and van Ranst designed a new Frontenac (upper illustration) with a Ballot-inspired 3-litre straight-eight engine. Twin overhead camshafts were driven by a train of gears, as on the 1920 engine, and Delco ignition was used on all the cars. Two straight-eights ran at Indianapolis in 1921, driven by Ralph Mulford and Tommy Milton. Milton won, a four-cylinder car driven by Jules Elingboe was third, and Mulford was ninth. Howard Wilcox won a short race at Indianapolis later in 1921, but after that the Frontenacs were outclassed by Duesenberg (88) and Miller, and had no further victories.

87 BALLOT, 1921, France

The first post-war Grand Prix Formula was for cars of 3 litres' capacity, and this limit fortunately applied also to Indianapolis. There was, in fact, no European Grand Prix racing in 1920, but for the American classic Ernest Henry designed a 3-litre straight-eight Ballot which was very similar in layout to the 1919 5-litre cars (82). The 1920 cars looked more modern, however, for the bolster tank of the earlier cars gave way to a long pointed tail with the spare wheel concealed within, in the manner of the 1914 Grand Prix Peugeots. They also had four-wheel brakes. Three of the new cars went to Indianapolis, to be driven by René Thomas, Jean Chassagne, and the American Ralph de Palma. As in 1919 the Ballots were the fastest cars in the race, and de Palma was leading at 450 miles when he stopped with magneto trouble. Thomas, who should have been behind him, had been delayed earlier by poor pit work, and victory went to the Monroe-Frontenac (86) of Gaston Chevrolet. Thomas was second, de Palma fifth, and Chassagne seventh. For the first post-war European Grand Prix, the 1921 race held at Le Mans, Ballot again entered three 3-litre cars, as well as a 2-litre which was the prototype of the 2LS production sports car. Drivers were Chassagne, de Palma, and Wagner on the 3-litre, and Goux on the smaller car. De Palma had the best car, but his lap times were slower than Chassagne and Wagner's. The reason for this was only revealed later when it was learnt that de Palma, always an opponent of four-wheel brakes, had the shoes secretly removed from the front wheels of his car. He finished second, behind Jimmy Murphy's Duesenberg (88), while Chassagne and Wagner both retired. Goux, surprisingly, was third in the 2-litre car. Later in 1921 Goux and Chassagne were first and second in the Italian Grand Prix, and Thomas second in the Targa Florio, all in 3-litre cars. In 1922 Goux and Foresti were second and third in the Targa Florio, in 2-litre Ballots, but the streamlined 2-litres which ran in the 1922 French Grand Prix at Strasbourg did not distinguish themselves. After that Ballot gave up Grand Prix racing to concentrate on building sports cars.

88 DUESENBERG, 1921, U.S.A.

The first eight-cylinder Duesenberg racing car appeared at Indianapolis in 1919, when Tommy Milton drove a 4·9-litre straight-eight with single overhead camshaft. As well as being the company's first eight it also marked the breakaway from the 'walking-beam' valve actuation which had characterized Duesenberg engines since the beginning (71). Milton's car retired at Indianapolis, and the 4·9-litre was replaced for 1920 by a 3-litre single overhead camshaft engine with three valves per cylinder, to conform with the new regulations. With these cars Milton, Jimmy Murphy, and Eddie Hearne finished third, fourth, and sixth at Indianapolis, and also had a number of successes on the board tracks such as Uniontown, Pennsylvania (Milton), Beverley Hills, California (Murphy), and Fresno, California (Murphy). In 1921 Duesenberg entered four cars for the French Grand Prix. They were similar to the 1920 models, but had hydraulic brakes on all four wheels, a system which had been introduced on the Model A passenger car. The drivers were Murphy, Albert Guyot, and Louis Inghibert, but the latter was badly injured in a practice crash and was replaced by the *aperitif* magnate André Dubonnet. The team manager was George Robertson, who had won the 1908 Vanderbilt Cup in a Locomobile (25). The Le Mans circuit was very rough and full of large stones, two of

the Duesenbergs suffering from these. Guyot's mechanic was hit on the head with one and so stunned that he could not crank the car, whereupon Arthur Duray who was in the Duesenberg pit took over as Guyot's mechanic. Murphy's car suffered a damaged radiator which leaked so badly that the engine was practically red-hot when he finished the race; but nevertheless he won. This was the first victory by an American car and driver in a European Grand Prix. Murphy later bought his car from the company and installed a Miller engine. In this form the car won the 1922 Indianapolis race. Duesenbergs were second, fourth, sixth, and eighth at Indianapolis in 1921, and also won board track races at Cotati and Beverley Hills, California, both with Eddie Hearne at the wheel. For 1922 the company developed a twin overhead camshaft head for the 3-litre cars, and in this form they filled five of the first seven places at Indianapolis. In 1923 the formula was reduced to 122 cu. in. (1990 cc.), and the 3-litre Duesenbergs were no longer eligible for major American Automobile Association races.

89 SUNBEAM, 1921, Great Britain

In 1920 Sunbeam merged with Talbot and Darracq to form the S.T.D. Group, and the first racing cars to be made under this merger appeared the next year. They had 3-litre twin overhead camshaft engines with aluminium blocks and dry sump lubrication. Four Zenith carburettors were used, and output was 108 b.h.p. at 4000 r.p.m. Three of these cars went to Indianapolis in May 1921, two from the Sunbeam works at Wolverhampton and one from the Darracq works at Suresnes. They were identical except for the radiators. Haibe's Sunbeam finished fifth, but the other two cars retired. The Sunbeam was the only European car in the first ten finishers. For the French Grand Prix a confusing variety of S.T.D. cars was entered, comprising two Sunbeams, two Talbots, and three Talbot-Darracqs. The Sunbeams were withdrawn altogether because of late preparation caused by a coal strike, the other S.T.D. cars were also withdrawn and then hastily re-entered, and eventually two English Talbots and two French Talbot-Darracqs reached the starting line. As at Indianapolis, they were identical except for radiators. They did not shine in the Grand Prix, the best position being André Boillot's fifth on a French-built car, followed by Kenelm Lee Guinness and Henry Segrave in seventh and eighth places on Talbots. Like the Duesenbergs the S.T.D. cars suffered from flying stones, Segrave's car sustaining a holed oil tank which his mechanic Moriceau plugged with cotton waste. They managed to complete the race before any fluff was sucked into the lubrication system. With some modifications, the 1921 Grand Prix cars ran in the 1922 Tourist Trophy, Jean Chassagne winning from Frank Clement in a 3-litre Bentley. The modifications included two Claudel Hobson carburettors in place of the four Zeniths and two magnetos in place of the Delco coil of the Grand Prix cars. Power was increased from 108 to 112 b.h.p. The 3-litre cars were also raced at Brooklands by Segrave and others, and one

was still racing on Southport sands as late as 1934.

90 FIAT, 1921, Italy

Fiat's first straight-eight racing car, the Tipo 802, was built for the 1921 Grand Prix season. It had a 3-litre twin overhead camshaft engine with roller-bearing crankshaft, which developed 120 b.h.p. at 4400 r.p.m. It was intended to enter a team in the French Grand Prix at Le Mans, but unfortunately the cars were not ready, and their first appearance was in the Italian Grand Prix at Brescia. The drivers were Louis Wagner, Pietro Bordino, and Ugo Sivocci. The latter crashed on the first lap, but Bordino led for thirteen laps, though slowed afterwards by tire troubles, and forced out of the race on the fifteenth lap by a broken oil connection. Wagner was also much troubled by having to make five wheel changes, and finished third, well behind two 3-litre Ballots (87). Bordino later took an 802 to America and won a number of board speedway events in 1922, including those at Cotati and Beverly Hills, California. Also in 1922 Biagio Nazzaro, nephew of the famous Felice who had driven Grand Prix Fiats before 1914, drove an 802 in the Targa Florio. This car (illustrated) abandoned the pointed tail of the original model for an old-fashioned bolster tank behind which the spare wheel was attached. Nazzaro was in third place on the first lap, but crashed on the second. He was not badly injured, but the news caused consternation among the crowds, who believed that it was his famous uncle who had crashed, and fatally at that.

The introduction of the 2-litre Grand Prix Formula for 1922 spelled the end of the 802, which was replaced by the much more successful Bertarione-designed six-cylinder Tipo 804.

91 AUSTRO-DAIMLER,
1921, Austria

In 1921 and 1922 the Austro-Daimler company supported an ambitious racing programme, with four types of car, all designed by Ferdinand Porsche. The two smaller models were known as the Saschas, after Count Sascha Kolowrat, a wealthy man who supported the racing team, at least of the smaller cars. These were of 1100-cc. and 1496-cc. capacity, while the larger cars were 2- and 3-litre models. The latter, known as the ADMR-6, was the only six-cylinder in the range. All had twin overhead camshaft engines with four valves per cylinder. The 3-litre car (illustrated) had an output of 109 b.h.p. at 4500 r.p.m. and a maximum speed of about 110 m.p.h. It was not raced very widely, as Austria, being an 'ex-enemy' country, was not allowed to take part in British or French events. The ban did not apply to Italy, which explains the large number of Mercedes, Steyr, Steiger, and other Teutonic cars in the Targa Florios of the early 20s, but although Austro-Daimler sent a team of Saschas to the 1922 Targa, they did not run the larger car there. The ADMR-6 took a number of hill-climb records, including the 3-litre class at Semmering with Alfred Neubauer at the wheel, and one came to Brooklands in 1926, where George Newman campaigned it with some success up to

1930, improving its maximum speed to 118 m.p.h. in the process. The celebrated hill-climb and racing driver Hans Stuck acquired an ADMR chassis into which he put a new six-cylinder Austro-Daimler engine in 1928, and had many hill-climb successes with it. The ADMR-4 was built in 1922 to take part in the 1923 Italian Grand Prix, but the team was withdrawn following a fatal accident to Fritz Kuhn when a wheel collapsed. This was the last straw for the Austro-Daimler management, who were opposed to racing anyway, and the works no longer supported sporting activities. Porsche left immediately and joined Mercedes, for whom he later designed the legendary SS and SSK sports cars.

92 CHITTY-BANG-BANG,
1921, Great Britain

Count Louis Vorow Zborowski was one of the most colourful characters at Brooklands in the early 1920s. Although he drove such cars as the 1914 Grand Prix Mercedes (77) and 4·9-litre Ballot (82), he realized that the fastest way to lap Brooklands was in an aero-engined car. The first such machine to appear at the track was the 350-h.p. Sunbeam (83), but Zborowski's Chitty-Bang-Bang was the first of the amateur-built aero-engined machines. Built in the workshops of Zborowski's country house, Higham Place, near Canterbury, Chitty I had a 23-litre, six-cylinder Maybach engine bought from the Aircraft Disposal Co. Ltd. This developed slightly over 300 b.h.p. at the leisurely speed of 1500 r.p.m., giving a top speed of about 125 m.p.h. The chassis was a lengthened pre-1914 Mercedes, while radiator, clutch and gear-box were also of Mercedes origin. Originally a four-seater body was fitted (upper illustration), with a crude exhaust pipe looking as if it had come from an ancient stove running the length of the body. Chitty was driven, on trade plates, from Canterbury to Brooklands in March 1921 for her first meeting, and won her first race, a 100 m.p.h. Short Handicap, at 100·75 m.p.h. Later that day she won the Lightning Short Handicap and came second in a Senior Sprint Race behind another of Zborowski's cars, the 1914 Grand Prix Mercedes. For the next Brooklands meeting Chitty had a new two-seater 'duck's back' body (lower illustration), a tidied-up exhaust system and guards over the driving chains. With a ten-second start she easily beat the 350-h.p. Sunbeam, and her handicap had to be revised several times in the ensuing months. Zborowski continued to race Chitty I up to the autumn of 1922, at Brooklands and at Southsea's Speed Trials, as well as using her on the road. At the Essex Motor Club Meeting at Brooklands in September 1922 Zborowski crashed, damaging Chitty, though without serious injury to himself. He never raced Chitty I again, as by that time he had built two successors, the 18·8-litre Chitty II and 14·7-litre shaft-driven Chitty III. After his death in 1924 Chitty I was bought by Captain J. E. P. Howey, then by the Conan Doyle brothers (sons of the creator of Sherlock Holmes) who ran her in one speed trial in the early 1930s. She was exhibited at Brooklands in 1934 and shortly afterwards was broken up. Chitty II still survives today.

93 HORSTMAN, 1921, Great Britain

The Horstman was one of the more unusual British light cars of the early 1920s. It was built by Sidney Horstmann at Bath, Somerset (up to 1921 the car as well as the designer was spelt Horstmann, but thereafter only one 'n' was used), and the original post-war model had a four-cylinder horizontal-valve engine of 1327 cc., made by Horstmann. This in itself was unusual in the days when most of the smaller car manufacturers used proprietary engines. It also featured a kick-starter operated from the driver's seat. For 1921 a Coventry-Simplex 1498-cc. side-valve engine was offered as an alternative, and a sports model with engine tuned to give 33·6 b.h.p. was available from mid-1921. Also in 1921 a racing car was built for Douglas Hawkes to drive in the Coupe des Voiturettes; this had a 1496-cc. Anzani engine, and front-wheel brakes. Hawkes did not finish among the leaders, but he drove the car again in the Junior Car Club's 200 Miles Race at Brooklands in October 1921. Also in the Horstmann team at Brooklands were three Coventry-Simplex-engined cars (illustrated), driven by Horstmann, C. F. Temple, and T. L. Edwards. They were much lower than the standard sports models, with longer tails and cowled radiators. Horstmann failed to start, Edwards retired after four laps, and Temple after eighteen laps, but Hawkes finished fifth at 82·37 m.p.h. This was very creditable when it is realized that the only cars ahead of him were the three works Talbot-Darracqs (95) and a Brescia Bugatti. The company did not enter the 1922 200 Miles

163

Race, but in 1923 Hawkes and Temple were there, the latter with a supercharged engine said to develop 55 b.h.p. He failed to finish, but Hawkes again was fifth. In 1924 three standard sports cars ran in the '200', as well as a special supercharged car driven by Major Coe and said to develop 80 b.h.p. at 4200 r.p.m. He finished twelfth, but the three sports cars did not complete the race. This was the last important race that Horstmans entered.

94 ASTON MARTIN, 1921, Great Britain

The Aston Martin first appeared during 1921 as a light sports car powered by a $1\frac{1}{2}$-litre Coventry-Simplex side-valve engine. Although the engines were made in Coventry they were finished in Robert Bamford's and Lionel Martin's small works in Kensington, London. A racing version, known as 'Bunny' (illustrated), appeared at Brooklands in May 1921, and was entered in the Coupe des Voiturettes at Le Mans in September. It was a rather ungainly-looking vehicle, with unstreamlined body and artillery wheels, but it had a maximum speed of about 85 m.p.h. and had a good record for reliability. B. S. Marshall finished sixth at Le Mans, and in the 200 Miles Race at Brooklands in October he finished ninth, ahead of an overhead-valve Aston Martin driven by Count Zborowski. 'Bunny' continued to run during 1922, and finished second in that year's 200 Miles Race. In 1923 the side-valve engine was replaced by a twin overhead camshaft unit which had been developed for the 1922 Grand

Prix Aston Martins. This sixteen-valve engine with shaft-driven camshafts was curiously reminiscent of the Henry-designed Peugeot and Ballot units, and the design was said to have been obtained from a Peugeot engineer, Marcel Grémillon. It developed 55 b.h.p. at 4500 r.p.m., and gave the car a maximum speed of 95 m.p.h. The Grand Prix Astons were much slimmer and more attractive-looking machines than 'Bunny', with wire wheels and front-wheel brakes. Neither car finished in the 1922 French Grand Prix at Strasbourg, nor in the 200 Miles Race, but Zborowski was second in the Penya Rhin Grand Prix in Spain in 1922 and 1923. On the whole the twin overhead camshaft engine was less reliable than the side-valve unit, being prone to magneto trouble and broken valve springs.

95 TALBOT-DARRACQ, 1921, France

Despite the complexity of the S.T.D. Group's racing cars, which ran as Sunbeams, Talbots, and Talbot-Darracqs on various occasions (89), as a general rule the larger cars were Sunbeams and the little $1\frac{1}{2}$-litre *voiturettes* were always known as Talbot-Darracqs. These were among the most successful racing cars of their era, and their run of victories between 1921 and 1925 was not rivalled until the appearance of the Type 35 Bugatti. Their four-cylinder sixteen-valve twin overhead camshaft engines were virtually one half of the 3-litre straight-eight Grand Prix engine (89), and developed 53 b.h.p. at 4000 r.p.m. Like the Grand

Prix engines, they had aluminium cylinder blocks with steel liners. Three of these *voiturettes* were entered in the 1921 Coupe des Voiturettes, driven by René Thomas, Kenelm Lee Guinness, and Henry Segrave. The combination of such experienced drivers with such promising cars made them favourites for the race, and in fact the three Talbot-Darracqs led from start to finish, changing order among themselves but never being threatened by any other contenders. The final order was Thomas, Guinness, and Segrave, the winner averaging 72·1 m.p.h. for the 279-mile race. The cars had another 1-2-3 victory in the first Junior Car Club 200 Miles Race at Brooklands in October, when the successful drivers were Segrave, Guinness, and Malcolm Campbell. For this race they were fitted with streamlined bodies and cowled radiators (lower illustration). Segrave's fastest lap was 97·65 m.p.h., and his average for the race 88·2 m.p.h. The French cars continued their victorious progress in 1922, winning the International 1500-cc. Race in the Isle of Man (Algernon Lee Guinness), the 200 Miles Race (Kenelm Lee Guinness), and coming first, second, and third in the Coupe des Voiturettes (Kenelm Lee Guinness, Divo, and Segrave). A new engine was designed for the 1923 *voiturettes*, with dimensions of 67 × 105 mm. (1481 cc.), only two valves per cylinder and magneto in place of coil ignition. They continued the marque's winning streak, Divo and Moriceau coming first and second in the Coupe des Voiturettes, and Dario Resta winning the Spanish Voiturette Cup on the new banked track at Sitges. These 1923 cars, which developed

70 b.h.p. at 5000 r.p.m., were designed by the ex-Fiat engineer Vincent Bertarione, who was also responsible for the 1923 Grand Prix Sunbeams. Superchargers were used in 1924 when power was up to 100 b.h.p., and victories that year included the Swiss Grand Prix (Kenelm Lee Guinness), the 200 Miles Race (George Duller), and the Grand Prix de l'Ouverture at Montlhéry (Jack Scales first, Segrave second, Edmond Bourlier third). They were still winning in 1925, although an attempt to run them in the French Touring Car Grand Prix with road equipment was a failure. For 1926 they were replaced by a twin overhead camshaft straight-eight Talbot-Darracq.

96   A.C., 1921, Great Britain

In February 1921 S. F. Edge of Napier fame joined the board of Autocarriers Ltd., a South London firm who had begun by making three-wheeled delivery vans and had progressed to light four-cylinder, four-wheeled cars called A.C. by 1914. Edge's arrival sparked off an interest in sport. The standard A.C. used a 1½-litre, four-cylinder Anzani or 2-litre, six-cylinder unit of the company's own design, and some racing cars were built using these engines. However, the most celebrated racing and record-breaking A.C.s used very special four-cylinder engines designed by John Weller, one of the founders of the company. These had single chain-driven overhead camshafts operating four inclined overhead valves per cylinder, and developed 55 b.h.p. from 1½-litres. They were fitted into special chassis with bevel rear axles in place of the worn type used on production A.C.s, and tubular front axles. Various types of single- and two-seater bodies were fitted, of which two are shown. The lower illustration is of the single-seater with which J. A. Joyce set up a number of records at Brooklands in 1922. These included the hour at 101·39 m.p.h., the first time that a 1½-litre car had exceeded 100 miles in one hour. The upper illustration shows a two-seater built for the 1921 200 Miles Race. Three of these ran in the race, driven by B. A. Davey, S. C. H. Davis, and Munday. None finished, but a near-standard Anzani-engined sports car driven by Stead finished eighth. The bodies of these streamlined A.C.s were designed and built by the Hawker Aircraft Company whose head, Harry Hawker, drove one at Brooklands in 1921. Among his achievements was the flying half-mile record at 105·14 m.p.h.

INDEX

Make	Model	Reference No. (colour)	Page No. (description)
Fiat	1914	75	152
Fiat	1921	90	161
Frontenac	1921	86	158
Gobron-Brillié	1903	14	116
Grégoire	1912	53	138
Hispano-Suiza	1910	47	134
Horstmann	1921	93	163
Hotchkiss	1906	24	122
Hutton	1908	42	131
Isotta-Fraschini	1908	44	132
Itala	1908	36	128
Itala	1913	70	149
Jeantaud	1898–99	3	110
La Jamais Contente	1899	2	109
Lion-Peugeot	1910	46	134
Locomobile	1906	25	123
Lorraine-Dietrich	1912	60	142
Martini	1907	33	127
Martini	1908	39	130
Mathis	1912	56	140
Mercedes	1903	17	118
Mercedes	1908	37	129
Mercedes	1914	77	153
Minerva	1907	34	128
Monroe-Frontenac	1920	86	158
Mors	60 hp	7	112
Nagant	1914	76	152
Napier	1902	11	114
Napier	1904	18	119
Napier	1908	35	128
Opel	1908	41	131
Opel	1914	78	154

Make	Model	Reference No. (colour)	Page No. (description)
Panhard	40 hp	6	112
Panhard	70 hp	10	114
Peugeot	1912	65	145
Peugeot	1920	85	158
Piccard-Pictet	1914	74	151
Pipe	1907	31	126
Premier	1916	81	155
Renault	16 hp	8	113
Renault	1906	26	123
Richard-Brasier	1904	19	119
Richard-Brasier	1905	19	119
Rolland-Pilain	1912	54	139
Schneider	1913	68	148
Serpollet	1902	12	115
Sizaire-Naudin	1912	62	143
Spyker	1902	9	113
Stanley	1906	22	121
Straker-Squire	1912	61	143
Straker-Squire	1918	82	156
Stutz	1915	80	155
Sunbeam	1911	48	135
Sunbeam	1912	64	144
Sunbeam	1914	79	154
Sunbeam	1920	84	157
Sunbeam	1921	89	160
Talbot	1913	67	147
Talbot-Darracq	1921	95	164
Thomas	1908	40	130
Vauxhall	1909	45	133
Vauxhall	1912	55	139
Violet-Bogey	1913	73	151
Winton	1903	13	115
Wolseley	1905	20	120